Writer and consultant Andrew Brooks
Senior editor Marie Greenwood
Senior designer Jim Green

Map illustrator Jeongeun Park
Illustrators Maltings Partnership,
Daniel Long
Senior editors Gill Pitts, Cécile Landau
Project art editor Hoa Luc
Designer Emma Hobson
Design assistant Rhea Gaughan
Cartography Ed Merritt, Simon Mumford
Index Helen Peters
Pre-production Dragana Puvacic
Production Srijana Gurung
Managing editor Laura Gilbert
Managing art editor Diane Peyton Jones
Art director Martin Wilson
Publisher Sarah Larter
Publishing director Sophie Mitchell

This edition published in 2021
First published in Great Britain in 2016 by
Dorling Kindersley Limited
DK, One Embassy Gardens, 8 Viaduct Gardens,
London, SW11 7BW

The authorised representative in the EEA is
Dorling Kindersley Verlag GmbH. Amulfstr. 124,
80636 Munich, Germany

Copyright © 2016, 2021 Dorling Kindersley Limited.
A Penguin Random House Company
10 9 8 7 6 5 4 3 2
032–196405–May/2021

A CIP catalogue record for this book
is available from the British Library
ISBN: 978-0-2412-2807-4

Printed in UAE

For the curious
www.dk.com

This book was made with Forest
Stewardship Council ™ certified paper –
one small step in DK's commitment to a
sustainable future. For more information
go to www.dk.com/our-green-pledge

CONTENTS

HOW TO READ THE MAPS

A map is a drawing that gives an instant impression of a place. The maps in this book show many of the world's countries plotted with rivers, mountains, forests, and plains.

Picture symbols
You will find picture symbols of a country's produce, industry, sports, and activities plotted on each country map. Look at the key to find what each symbol means

Picture features
Pictures with text pick out a country's special features, including historic sites, animals, and natural wonders

Capital
A country's capital city is marked with a red outline

Bordering countries
Around the edges of the map you can see all the bordering countries

FRANCE

France is known throughout the world for its food and wine and beautiful countryside. Today, most French people live in towns and cities. France is highly industrialized and has one of the fastest train networks, the TGV. The arts, such as painting, and sport, particularly cycling, are very popular.

Flag
On every country, you'll find the country's flag

History and culture
These photographs show historical and cultural features that are unique to that country

Places of interest
These photographs zoom in on a city, building, or landscape and show where it is on the map

Produce
Close-up photographs show food, drink, and other goods that a country produces

Page numbers
The colour of the circle matches the continent opener and tells you which continent you are in

On the map:

UNITED KINGDOM

BELGIUM

Channel Tunnel

Lille

Calais

Vimy Memorial

ENGLISH CHANNEL

Lens

This medieval tapestry shows the story of the Norman conquest of England in 1066

Rouen

Reims

This monument all the Canadi lives in the wa

Bayeux Tapestry

Le Havre

Eiffel Tower

Seine

People can walk to the abbey and houses on this island during low tides

Mont-Saint-Michel

Completed in 1889, this iron tower is 324 m (1,063 ft) tall including the TV antenna that was added to the top

Paris

About 3,000 big stones were placed in rows at this ancient site more than 5,000 years ago

Le Mans

This is the largest and grandest château in the Loire

Orléans

Dijon is famous for its mustard, which was first made here in 1856

Dijo

Art
Millions of people visit France's museums every year to see paintings and sculptures by artists such as Claude Monet and Auguste Rodin.

Water Lilies, by Monet

Rennes

Nantes

Carnac stones

Loire

Château de Chambord

FRANCE

Saône

Loire châteaux
The Loire Valley is famous for its 42 châteaux, or large country houses. Château de Chenonceau sits across the River Cher on a row of arches.

ATLANTIC OCEAN

Volcanoes in this nature park last erupted 6,000 years ago

Volcans d'Auvergne

MASSIF CENTRAL

Lyon

Humans painted horses and wild cattle on cave walls more than 17,000 years ago

Lascaux caves

The Romans built this aqueduct bridge to transport water across the river

St Étienne

Bonjour! Hello

Dordogne

Garonne

Périgord truffles

Millau Viaduct

Pont d

Cheese and wine
More than 400 different cheeses are made in France. Almost every area has its own type, ranging from soft cheeses, such as Camembert, to hard and even blue cheeses. France also produces some of the world's best wines, made from the juice of black or white grapes. Sunflowers are also grown in the south. Their seeds are pressed to make oil.

Bears from Slovenia were moved to the Pyrenees after the last local bear died in 2006

These edible fungi sell for hundreds of pounds a kilo

The world's highest bridge is 343 m (1,125 ft) – even taller than the Eiffel Tower

Bordeaux

Toulouse

Brown bear

Flamingos

Montpellier

Sunflower

Grapes

Camembert cheese

PYRENEES

Perpignan

Flamingos siev water through bills to feed o animals and p

SPAIN

ANDORRA

SCALE
0   50 miles   100 miles
0   100 kilometres

58

Language
You will find speech bubbles that say "Hello" or "Goodbye" in the country's main language

Scale
The scale indicates the size of the country and the distances between different points on the map

Cities
Towns and cities featured on the map are marked with a blue outline

Rivers
A country's most important rivers are shown on each map

Country borders

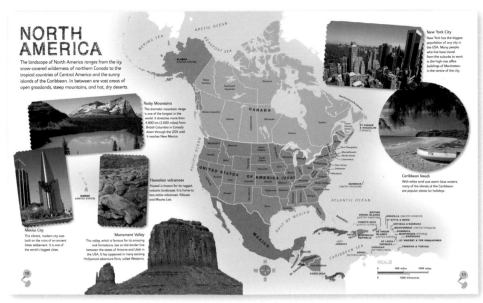

Borders
The borders between countries are shown with a red broken line.

Disputed borders
Some countries disagree about where the border between them should be. These borders are shown with a dotted line.

Compass
The compass always points north (N) in line with the map and also shows the direction of south (S), east (E), and west (W)

Au revoir!
Goodbye

Strasbourg

Outdoor markets
Every French village and town has an outdoor market that opens at least one day a week. People can buy fresh fruit and vegetables grown at nearby farms and local produce, such as cheese.

French street market

Café culture
French people enjoy meeting up with their friends in cafés. They often have a croissant (a flaky pastry) and coffee for breakfast. In the evenings, popular drinks include beer, wine, or champagne (a fizzy wine).

A popular café in Paris

ats live slopes.

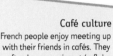

Tour de France
The world's most famous bicycle race lasts for three weeks and passes through the Alps and Pyrenees before finishing in Paris.

Alpine ibex

oble

KEY

PRODUCE
- Vineyards
- Sunflowers
- Beef cattle
- Wheat
- Apples
- Cheese
- Champagne
- Shellfish
- Pigs

INDUSTRY
- Nuclear power
- Aircraft manufacture
- Fishing
- Cars

ACTIVITIES
- Mountain climbing
- Skiing
- Cycling
- Surfing

Nice

Monaco is a small country that is independent from France

MONACO

TGV

Toulon

French Riviera

eille

al-wild horses he marshes o argue

High-speed trains connect France's major cities

The southeast coast is famous for its seaside resorts and the Cannes Film Festival

Napoleon Bonaparte was born in Corsica in 1769. He became Emperor of France in 1804 and died in 1821

Corsica

59

MEDITERRANEAN SEA

Independent states
Small independent states, such as Monaco, are shown with a red border and a solid red dot, and the name is in capital letters.

Key
Every country map has a key listing major features, such as produce and industry, that relate to the picture symbols on the map

---

NORTH AMERICA

The landscape of North America ranges from the icy, snow-covered wilderness of northern Canada to the tropical countries of Central America and the sunny islands of the Caribbean. In between are vast areas of open grasslands, steep mountains, and hot, dry deserts.

New York City
New York has the biggest population of any city in the USA. Many people who live here travel from the suburbs to work in the high-rise office buildings of Manhattan in the centre of the city.

Rocky Mountains
This dramatic mountain range is one of the longest in the world. It stretches more than 4,800 km (3,000 miles) from British Columbia in Canada down through the USA until it reaches New Mexico.

Hawaiian volcanoes
Hawaii is known for its rugged, volcanic landscape. It is home to two active volcanoes: Kilauea and Mauna Loa.

Caribbean beach
With white sand and warm blue waters, many of the islands of the Caribbean are popular places for holidays.

Mexico City
This vibrant, modern city was built on the ruins of an ancient Aztec settlement. It is one of the world's biggest cities.

Monument Valley
This valley, which is famous for its amazing rock formations, lies on the border line between the states of Arizona and Utah in the USA. It has appeared in many exciting Hollywood adventure films, called Westerns.

SCALE
500 miles   1000 miles
1000 kilometres

Continent maps

The continent maps are coloured to show every country in each continent. Photographs show the continent's major features.

Habitats

These colours and symbols show the different habitats, or landscapes, of each country.

Hot deserts
Hot deserts are dry and sandy areas and few plants grow here.

Cold deserts
Cold deserts, such as the Gobi in Asia, are cold, dry stretches of land.

Snow and ice
Frozen areas are found high up in the mountains and near the North and South Poles.

Mountains
High, rugged mountainous areas are often covered with snow.

Oceans and seas
Huge stretches of water surround the seven continents.

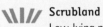
Scrubland
Low-lying plants and grasses grow in scrubland areas, such as in southern Spain.

Wetland
Wetlands are marshy, swampy areas, such as the Pantanal in Brazil.

Grassland
Grasslands are flat, grassy plains with few trees, such as the savanna of Africa

Tropical
Rainforests, such as the Amazon, get a lot of rain and so the trees grow very tall.

Deciduous forests
These forests have trees that lose their leaves in the autumn and winter.

Coniferous forests
Evergreen trees that do not lose their leaves in winter are found in coniferous forests.

NORTH AMERICA

North America
This huge continent lies wholly in the northern half (hemisphere) of the world. It includes Greenland, which lies above the Arctic Circle.

ATLANTIC OCEAN

Equator
This is an imaginary line that goes round the middle of the Earth, dividing it into two halves, called the north and south hemispheres.

PACIFIC OCEAN

South America
This continent lies mainly in the southern hemisphere of the world. North, Central, and South America are together known as the Americas.

SOUTH AMERICA

ATLANTIC OCEAN

THE WORLD

This is a flat map of our round Earth. Land covers about a third of Earth's surface. This land is broken up into seven large blocks called continents. Water makes up the rest of the Earth and is divided into five major areas, called oceans.

Antarctica
This is the most southern of all the continents. It is covered in frozen ice and hardly anybody lives here.

SOUTHERN OCEAN

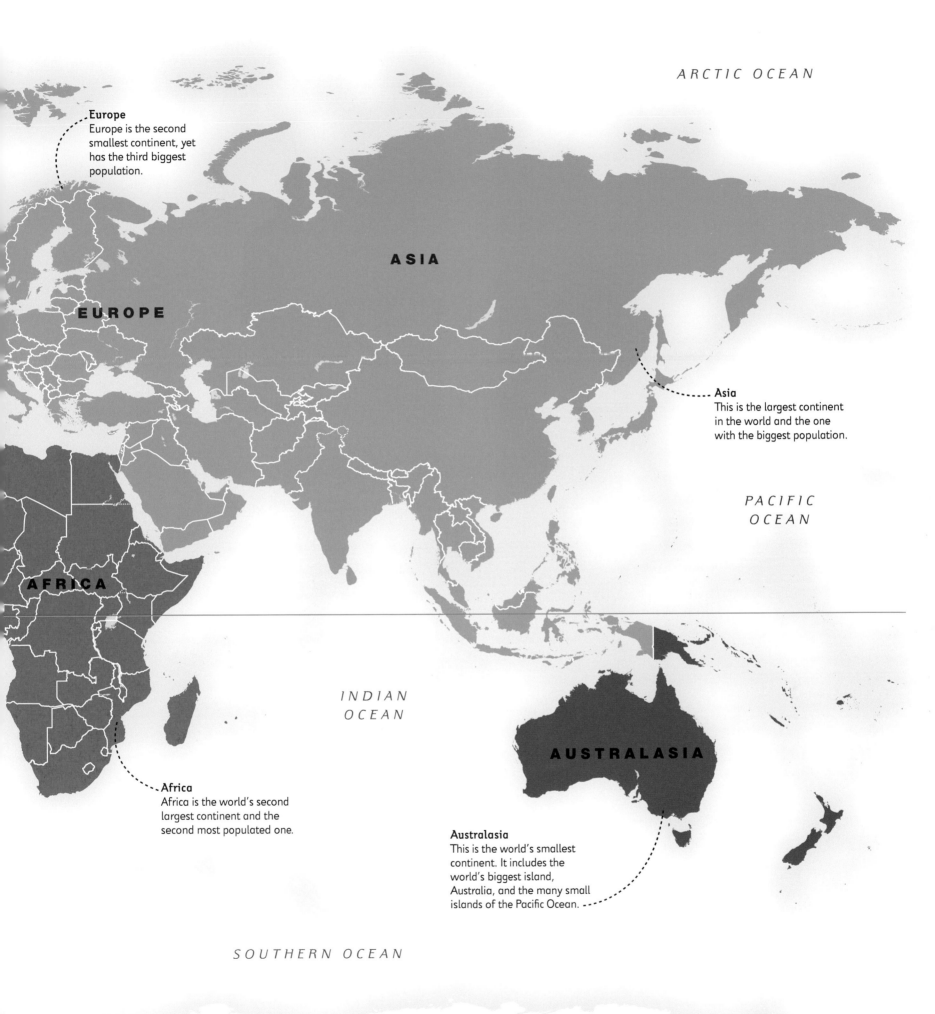

Europe
Europe is the second smallest continent, yet has the third biggest population.

ASIA

EUROPE

Asia
This is the largest continent in the world and the one with the biggest population.

PACIFIC OCEAN

AFRICA

Africa
Africa is the world's second largest continent and the second most populated one.

INDIAN OCEAN

AUSTRALASIA

Australasia
This is the world's smallest continent. It includes the world's biggest island, Australia, and the many small islands of the Pacific Ocean.

SOUTHERN OCEAN

ANTARCTICA

2. The merengue is the national dance of which Caribbean country?

3. In which Canadian city is the CN Tower found?

1. Which mountain is this sculpture carved into?

4. In which country would you find this ancient Pyramid of the Sun?

NORTH AMERICA

Canada, the United States of America (USA), Mexico, Central America, and the Caribbean islands make up North America. This vast continent was first settled by American Indian people before the arrival of Europeans and people from other parts of the world.

8. Which canal connects the world's two biggest oceans?

7. Who were the first people to settle in northern Canada?

6. Which river flows through the Grand Canyon?

5. In which American city will you see yellow taxis?

You can find all the answers and more quizzes on pages 120–121.

NORTH AMERICA

The landscape of North America ranges from the icy, snow-covered wilderness of northern Canada to the tropical countries of Central America and the sunny islands of the Caribbean. In between are vast areas of open grasslands, steep mountains, and hot, dry deserts.

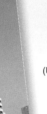

Rocky Mountains

This dramatic mountain range is one of the longest in the world. It stretches more than 4,800 km (3,000 miles) from British Columbia in Canada down through the USA until it reaches New Mexico.

Hawaiian volcanoes

Hawaii is known for its rugged, volcanic landscape. It is home to two active volcanoes: Kilauea and Mauna Loa.

Mexico City

This vibrant, modern city was built on the ruins of an ancient Aztec settlement. It is one of the world's biggest cities.

Monument Valley

This valley, which is famous for its amazing rock formations, lies on the border line between the states of Arizona and Utah in the USA. It has appeared in many exciting Hollywood adventure films, called Westerns.

ARCTIC OCEAN

BERING SEA

BEAUFORT SEA

ALASKA
(UNITED STATES)

Yukon Territory

Northwest Territories

British Columbia

Alberta

PACIFIC OCEAN

Washington

Montana

Oregon

Idaho

UNITED STATES

Nevada

Utah

California

Arizona

HAWAII
(UNITED STATES)

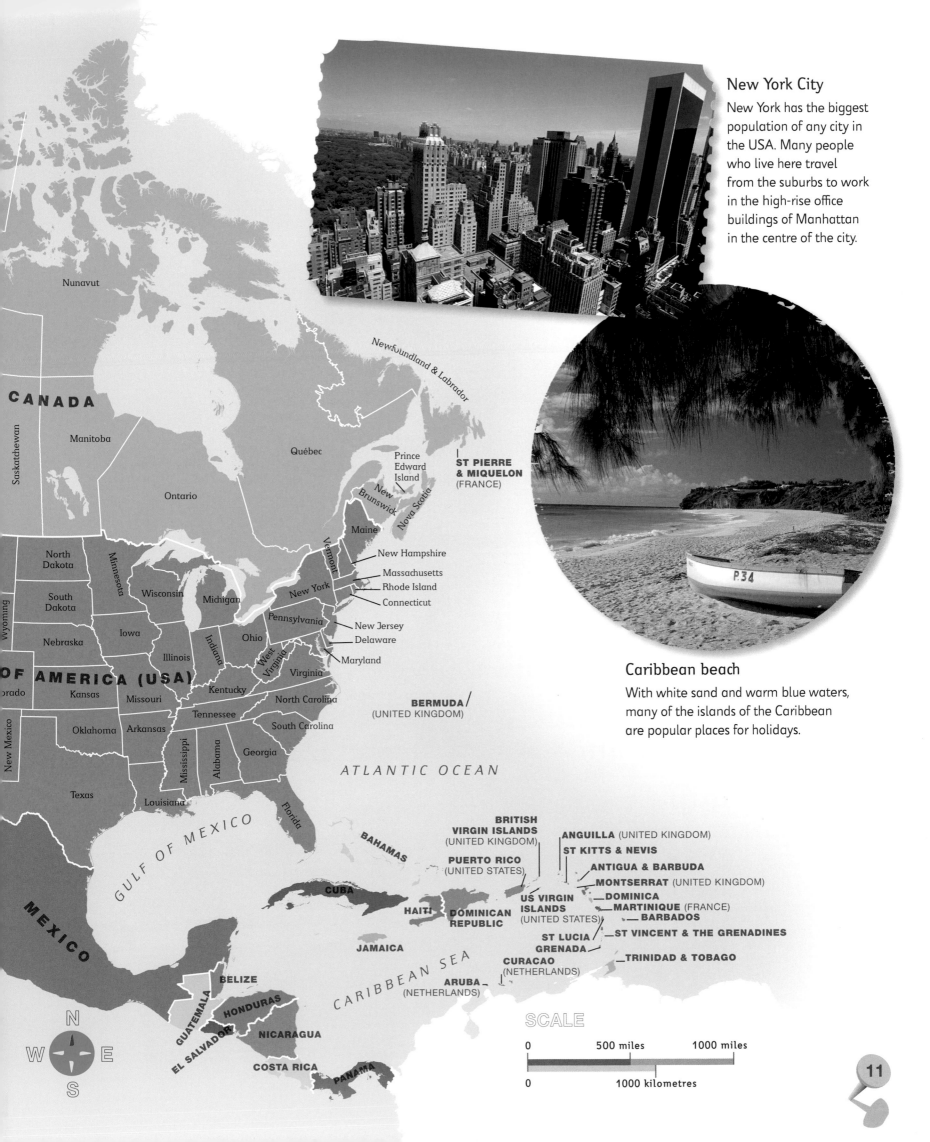

New York City

New York has the biggest population of any city in the USA. Many people who live here travel from the suburbs to work in the high-rise office buildings of Manhattan in the centre of the city.

Caribbean beach

With white sand and warm blue waters, many of the islands of the Caribbean are popular places for holidays.

Nunavut

CANADA

Saskatchewan

Manitoba

Ontario

Québec

Newfoundland & Labrador

Prince Edward Island

New Brunswick

Nova Scotia

ST PIERRE & MIQUELON (FRANCE)

Maine

New Hampshire

Massachusetts

Rhode Island

Connecticut

Vermont

New York

Pennsylvania

New Jersey

Delaware

Maryland

North Dakota

South Dakota

Minnesota

Wisconsin

Michigan

Iowa

Illinois

Indiana

Ohio

West Virginia

Virginia

Wyoming

Nebraska

OF AMERICA (USA)

Kansas

Missouri

Kentucky

Tennessee

North Carolina

South Carolina

orado

New Mexico

Oklahoma

Arkansas

Mississippi

Alabama

Georgia

Texas

Louisiana

Florida

BERMUDA (UNITED KINGDOM)

ATLANTIC OCEAN

GULF OF MEXICO

M E X I C O

BAHAMAS

CUBA

HAITI

DOMINICAN REPUBLIC

JAMAICA

BRITISH VIRGIN ISLANDS (UNITED KINGDOM)

PUERTO RICO (UNITED STATES)

US VIRGIN ISLANDS (UNITED STATES)

ANGUILLA (UNITED KINGDOM)

ST KITTS & NEVIS

ANTIGUA & BARBUDA

MONTSERRAT (UNITED KINGDOM)

DOMINICA

MARTINIQUE (FRANCE)

BARBADOS

ST LUCIA

GRENADA

ST VINCENT & THE GRENADINES

CURACAO (NETHERLANDS)

ARUBA (NETHERLANDS)

TRINIDAD & TOBAGO

CARIBBEAN SEA

BELIZE

GUATEMALA

HONDURAS

EL SALVADOR

NICARAGUA

COSTA RICA

PANAMA

N W E S

SCALE

| 0 | 500 miles | 1000 miles |

| 0 | 1000 kilometres |

11

CANADA AND ALASKA

Canada is the world's second largest country. It has huge mountain ranges, wide and vast forests, and bustling cities. It is also rich in oil and mineral resources, as is Alaska, the biggest state in the USA.

Defending the net

Ice hockey
This fast-moving sport is very popular in Canada and can be played on ice rinks or frozen lakes. Both the women's and men's teams have won more Olympic gold medals than any other nation.

ARCTIC OCEAN

Grizzly bear
In the rivers of Alaska and western Canada, grizzly bears catch salmon as the fish swim and leap upstream in the autumn.

BEAUFORT SEA

Oil is carried across Alaska from the north coast to the south by the Trans-Alaska Pipeline

Prudhoe Bay

Trans-Alaska Pipeline

Alaska (USA) Yukon

At 6,190 m (20,310 ft) Denali is the highest mountain in North America

Mackenzie

The Inuit were the first people to settle in north Canada; they play drums at special events and celebrations

Inuit drummers

Great Bear Lake

Fairbanks

Line fishing

Denali

Anchorage

Valdez

ROCKY MOUNTAINS

Pelly

Yellowknife

The Mounties police force wear red jackets on special occasions

Great Slave Lake

Alaskan rivers are full of trout and other fish

Sea otter

The Alaskan coast is home to groups of sea otters, which rest floating on their backs

Whitehorse

Juneau

COAST MOUNTAINS

Canadian Mountie

More than one million people come to this big rodeo festival every July

Calgary Stampede

Edmonton

KEY

PRODUCE
- Wheat
- Maize
- Dried beans and pulses

INDUSTRY
- Gold
- Coal
- Silver
- Oil
- Timber
- Uranium
- Technology
- Aircraft
- Gas
- Fishing
- Diamonds
- Aluminium
- Paper mill
- Cars

ACTIVITIES
- Hiking
- Skiing

PACIFIC OCEAN

Haida portrait figures made from wood

Haida figurines

Vancouver coast
Vancouver is an exciting, international city that is surrounded by nature. It is often voted as one of the best places in the world to live.

The first people of Canada carved wooden totem poles to show their cultural beliefs

Totem pole

Curling

Victoria

Vancouver

Calgary

Dinosaur Provincial Park

This sport is played with sliding stones on a sheet of ice

Well-preserved dinosaur fossils have been found in this park

First people
The Haida were among the first people to live in Canada before the arrival of Europeans. "Haida" means "person", and they live on the Pacific Northwest Coast.

SCALE
0 — 250 miles

0 — 250 kilometres

12

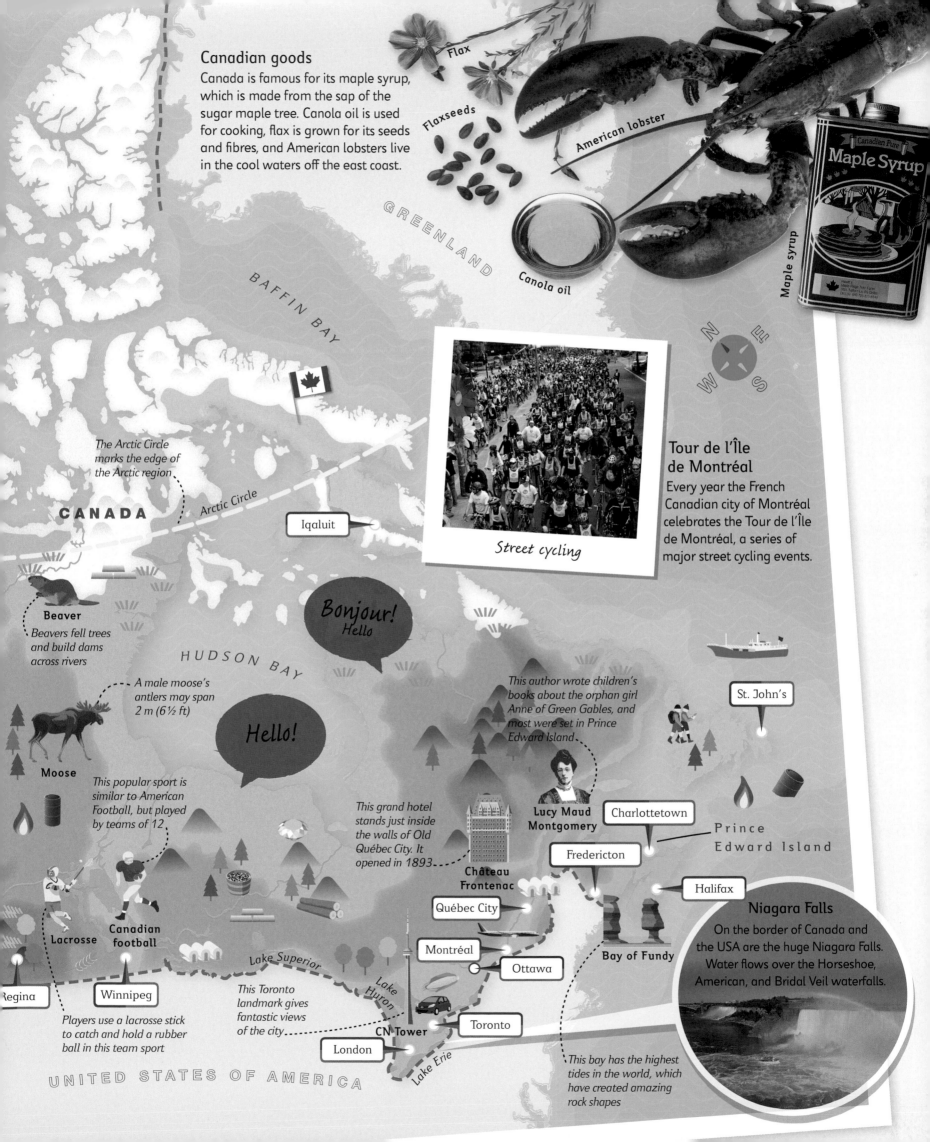

Canadian goods

Canada is famous for its maple syrup, which is made from the sap of the sugar maple tree. Canola oil is used for cooking, flax is grown for its seeds and fibres, and American lobsters live in the cool waters off the east coast.

Flax

Flaxseeds

American lobster

Maple Syrup
Canadian Pure

Canola oil

Maple syrup

GREENLAND

BAFFIN BAY

The Arctic Circle marks the edge of the Arctic region

CANADA

Arctic Circle

Iqaluit

Street cycling

Tour de l'Île de Montréal

Every year the French Canadian city of Montréal celebrates the Tour de l'Île de Montréal, a series of major street cycling events.

Beaver
Beavers fell trees and build dams across rivers

Bonjour!
Hello

HUDSON BAY

A male moose's antlers may span 2 m (6½ ft)

Hello!

Moose

This popular sport is similar to American Football, but played by teams of 12

This author wrote children's books about the orphan girl Anne of Green Gables, and most were set in Prince Edward Island

St. John's

Lucy Maud Montgomery

Charlottetown

This grand hotel stands just inside the walls of Old Québec City. It opened in 1893

Château Frontenac

Fredericton

Prince Edward Island

Halifax

Lacrosse

Canadian football

Québec City

Montréal

Bay of Fundy

Niagara Falls

On the border of Canada and the USA are the huge Niagara Falls. Water flows over the Horseshoe, American, and Bridal Veil waterfalls.

Regina

Winnipeg

Lake Superior

This Toronto landmark gives fantastic views of the city

Ottawa

Lake Huron

Players use a lacrosse stick to catch and hold a rubber ball in this team sport

CN Tower

Toronto

London

Lake Erie

UNITED STATES OF AMERICA

This bay has the highest tides in the world, which have created amazing rock shapes

Golden Gate Bridge

This huge suspension bridge spans the Golden Gate strait (narrow sea channel) between San Francisco Bay and the Pacific Ocean. It is San Francisco's most famous landmark.

Bald eagle

This large majestic eagle is a symbol of the USA

CANADA

SCALE

0 — 200 miles

0 — 200 kilometres

Seattle

R O C K Y   M O U N T A I N S

Columbia

Yellowstone is the world's oldest national park and inside the park is a huge geyser called "Old Faithful"

This sculpture carved into a mountain shows the faces of four US presidents

GREAT PLAINS

Yellowstone National Park

G R E A T

B A S I N

D E S E R T

Snake

Big, powerful bison once roamed the plains in large herds

American bison

Mount Rushmore

This is the highest waterfall in Yosemite National Park

UNITED STATES

Cable cars run up and down the steep hills of San Francisco

Salt Lake City

Denver

These golden-leaved trees grow throughout North America

Tornado Alley is so named because lots of tornadoes (huge whirlwinds) occur here

San Francisco

Cable cars

Yosemite Falls

Quaking aspen

PACIFIC OCEAN

Giant sequoia trees grow in this national park

Sequoia National Park

Stars fixed into the pavements of Hollywood celebrate famous entertainers

This steep-sided canyon was carved by the Colorado River

Santa Fe

Hollywood's Walk of Fame

Grand Canyon

Colorado

Cowboys are skilled horse riders who herd cattle

Tornado Alley

Los Angeles

This is Walt Disney's original theme park; it features rides, displays, and characters from Disney films

Disneyland Park

Phoenix

San Diego

Rio Grande

Pecos

Cowboy

Pueblo Eagle Dance

This dance performed by the Pueblo people of Colorado represents the flight of eagles

Navajo girls in traditional clothes

Native Americans

Native Americans were the first people to live in America. The Navajo, from Arizona and New Mexico, are the largest tribe.

USA

The United States of America (USA) is a huge and powerful country with 50 states. It has wide stretches of wilderness as well as big, modern cities. The landscape is a mix of vast plains, high mountain ranges, deserts, and wetlands. Many people from all over the world have made their home here.

Hawaii

The Pacific Ocean islands of Hawaii became the 50th state of the USA in 1959

Honolulu

H a w a i i

MEXICO

Aloha! Hello or goodbye

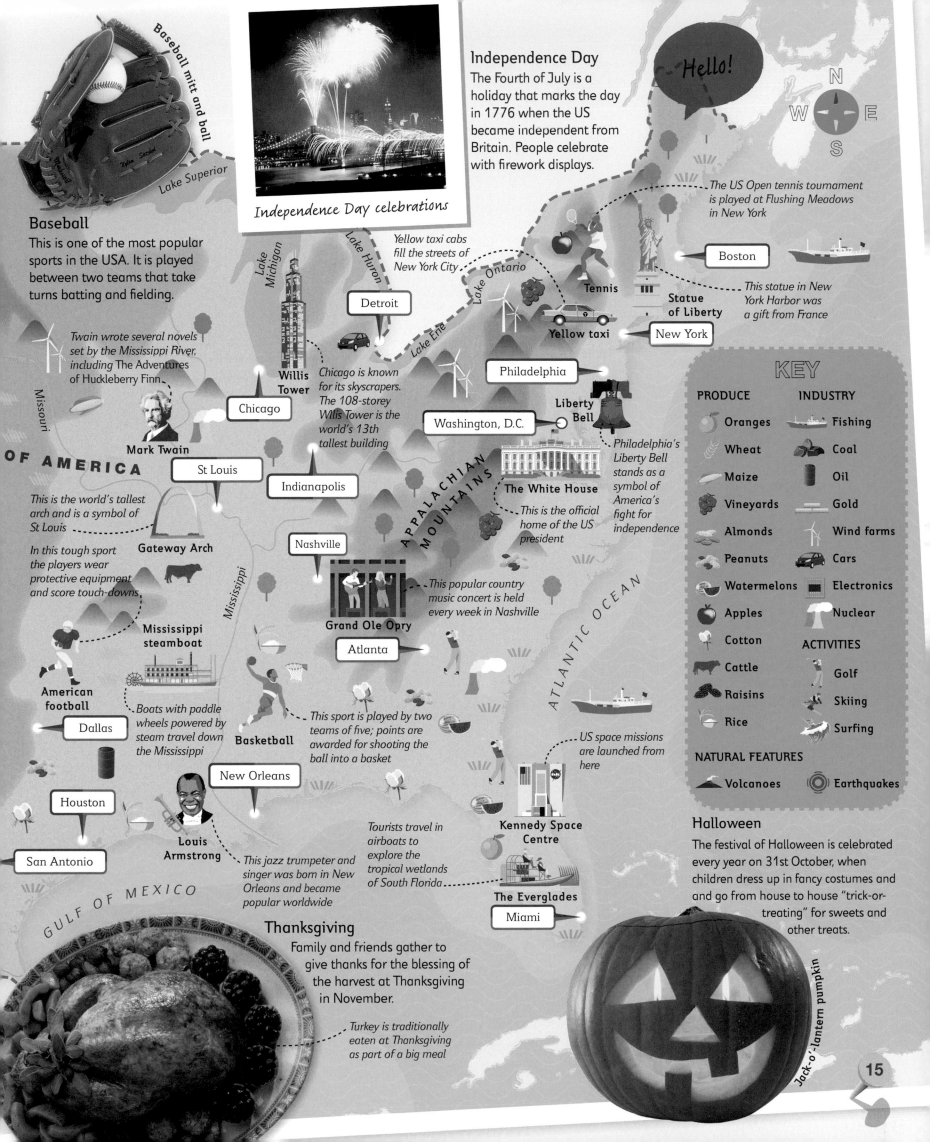

Baseball mitt and ball

Baseball

This is one of the most popular sports in the USA. It is played between two teams that take turns batting and fielding.

Independence Day celebrations

Independence Day

The Fourth of July is a holiday that marks the day in 1776 when the US became independent from Britain. People celebrate with firework displays.

Hello!

Lake Superior

The US Open tennis tournament is played at Flushing Meadows in New York

Boston

This statue in New York Harbor was a gift from France

Yellow taxi cabs fill the streets of New York City

Lake Michigan

Lake Huron

Lake Ontario

Lake Erie

Detroit

Tennis

Statue of Liberty

Yellow taxi

New York

Twain wrote several novels set by the Mississippi River, including The Adventures of Huckleberry Finn

Willis Tower

Philadelphia

Liberty Bell

Mark Twain

Chicago

Chicago is known for its skyscrapers. The 108-storey Willis Tower is the world's 13th tallest building

Washington, D.C.

Missouri

OF AMERICA

St Louis

Indianapolis

The White House

Philadelphia's Liberty Bell stands as a symbol of America's fight for independence

This is the world's tallest arch and is a symbol of St Louis

In this tough sport the players wear protective equipment and score touch-downs

Gateway Arch

APPALACHIAN MOUNTAINS

This is the official home of the US president

Nashville

Mississippi

Mississippi steamboat

Grand Ole Opry

This popular country music concert is held every week in Nashville

ATLANTIC OCEAN

American football

Atlanta

Dallas

Boats with paddle wheels powered by steam travel down the Mississippi

Basketball

This sport is played by two teams of five; points are awarded for shooting the ball into a basket

US space missions are launched from here

New Orleans

Houston

Louis Armstrong

San Antonio

This jazz trumpeter and singer was born in New Orleans and became popular worldwide

Tourists travel in airboats to explore the tropical wetlands of South Florida

Kennedy Space Centre

The Everglades

Miami

KEY

PRODUCE
- Oranges
- Wheat
- Maize
- Vineyards
- Almonds
- Peanuts
- Watermelons
- Apples
- Cotton
- Cattle
- Raisins
- Rice

INDUSTRY
- Fishing
- Coal
- Oil
- Gold
- Wind farms
- Cars
- Electronics
- Nuclear

ACTIVITIES
- Golf
- Skiing
- Surfing

NATURAL FEATURES
- Volcanoes
- Earthquakes

Halloween

The festival of Halloween is celebrated every year on 31st October, when children dress up in fancy costumes and and go from house to house "trick-or-treating" for sweets and other treats.

GULF OF MEXICO

Thanksgiving

Family and friends gather to give thanks for the blessing of the harvest at Thanksgiving in November.

Turkey is traditionally eaten at Thanksgiving as part of a big meal

Jack-o'-lantern pumpkin

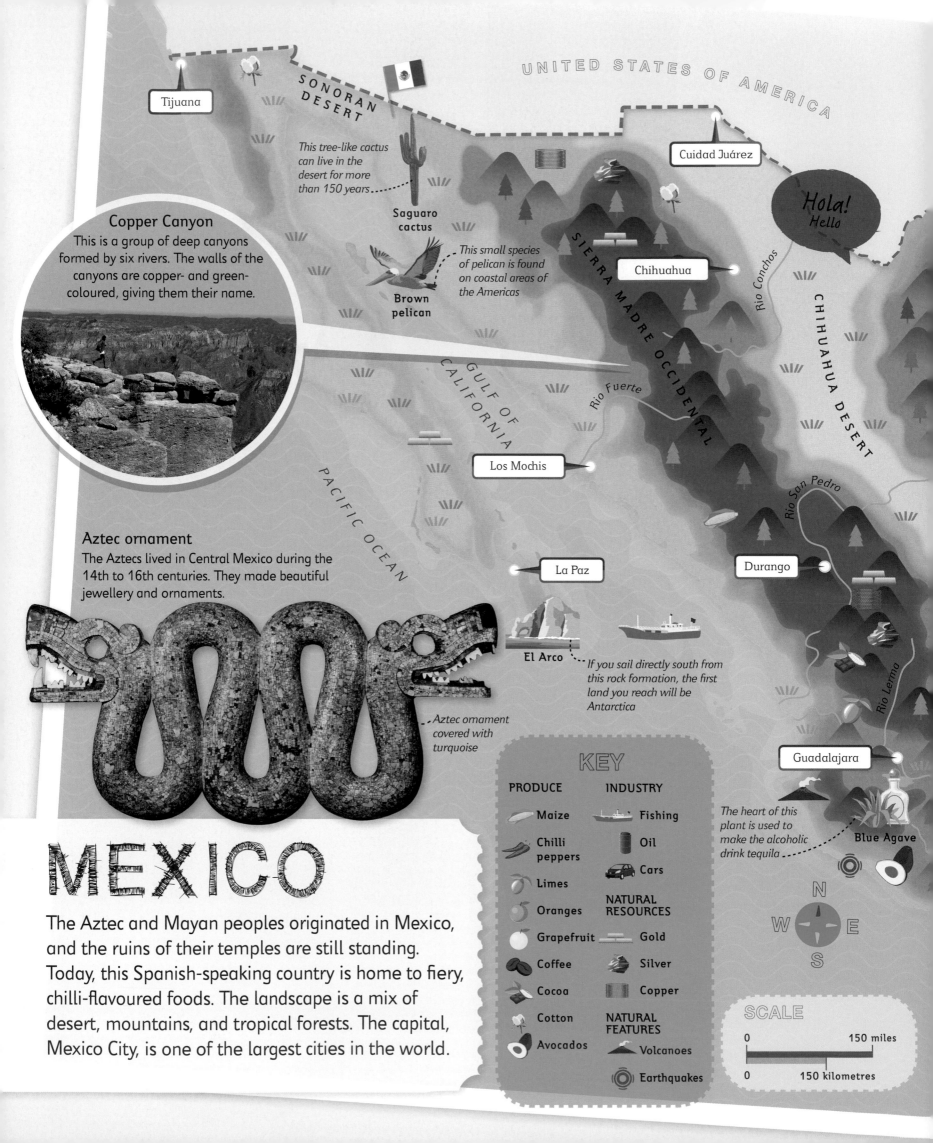

UNITED STATES OF AMERICA

Tijuana

SONORAN DESERT

This tree-like cactus
can live in the
desert for more
than 150 years

Saguaro
cactus

This small species
of pelican is found
on coastal areas of
the Americas

Brown
pelican

Cuidad Juárez

Hola!
Hello

Rio Conchos

Chihuahua

SIERRA MADRE OCCIDENTAL

CHIHUAHUA DESERT

Copper Canyon
This is a group of deep canyons
formed by six rivers. The walls of the
canyons are copper- and green-
coloured, giving them their name.

GULF OF CALIFORNIA

Rio Fuerte

Los Mochis

PACIFIC OCEAN

Rio San Pedro

Aztec ornament
The Aztecs lived in Central Mexico during the
14th to 16th centuries. They made beautiful
jewellery and ornaments.

La Paz

Durango

El Arco

If you sail directly south from
this rock formation, the first
land you reach will be
Antarctica

Rio Lerma

Aztec ornament
covered with
turquoise

Guadalajara

The heart of this
plant is used to
make the alcoholic
drink tequila

Blue Agave

KEY

PRODUCE	INDUSTRY
Maize	Fishing
Chilli peppers	Oil
Limes	Cars
Oranges	NATURAL RESOURCES
Grapefruit	Gold
Coffee	Silver
Cocoa	Copper
Cotton	NATURAL FEATURES
Avocados	Volcanoes
	Earthquakes

N
W E
S

MEXICO

The Aztec and Mayan peoples originated in Mexico,
and the ruins of their temples are still standing.
Today, this Spanish-speaking country is home to fiery,
chilli-flavoured foods. The landscape is a mix of
desert, mountains, and tropical forests. The capital,
Mexico City, is one of the largest cities in the world.

SCALE

0 ——————— 150 miles

0 ——————— 150 kilometres

Butterfly reserve

Every year in the autumn, thousands of monarch butterflies migrate (move) from northern North America to Mexico. The Monarch Butterfly Biosphere Reserve, northwest of Mexico City, protects these butterflies during the winter.

Monarch butterflies

Tacos

Limes

Spicy food

Mexican food is often very spicy and includes tacos, which are maize tortillas (soft flatbread) filled with meat or seafood. Refreshing limes and creamy avocados are grown in many parts of Mexico.

Avocados

Lucha Libre

Lucha Libre, which means "free wrestling", is a special type of wrestling. Fighters wear dramatic costumes, including masks, to hide their identity.

Masked wrestlers

Boxing is a major sport and Mexico has produced many world champion boxers

SIERRA MADRE ORIENTAL

Rio Grande

Boxing

Monterrey

MEXICO

GULF OF MEXICO

Armadillos are protected by their bony armour and leathery skin

Armadillo

Palenque

This ruined Mayan city in southern Mexico thrived from 500–700 CE. Many of the ruins are still covered by jungle.

Cancún

El Castillo

This temple was built by the Mayan civilization more than 1,000 years ago

This pyramid is one of the largest ancient buildings in the Americas

León

Campeche

Veracruz

Pyramid of the Sun

Puebla

These giant stone heads were carved 3,000 years ago

This volcano is the highest mountain in Mexico

Metropolitan Cathedral

Mexico City

YUCATAN PENINSULA

GUATEMALA

BELIZE

Skeleton puppet

Pico de Orizaba

Acapulco

Olmec heads

This is the largest cathedral in the Americas

Oaxaca

These sweets in the shape of skulls are given to celebrate the Day of the Dead

Day of the Dead

On this Mexican holiday, family and friends gather to pray and remember people who have died. Parades are held and colourful puppets are made in the shape of skeletons.

17

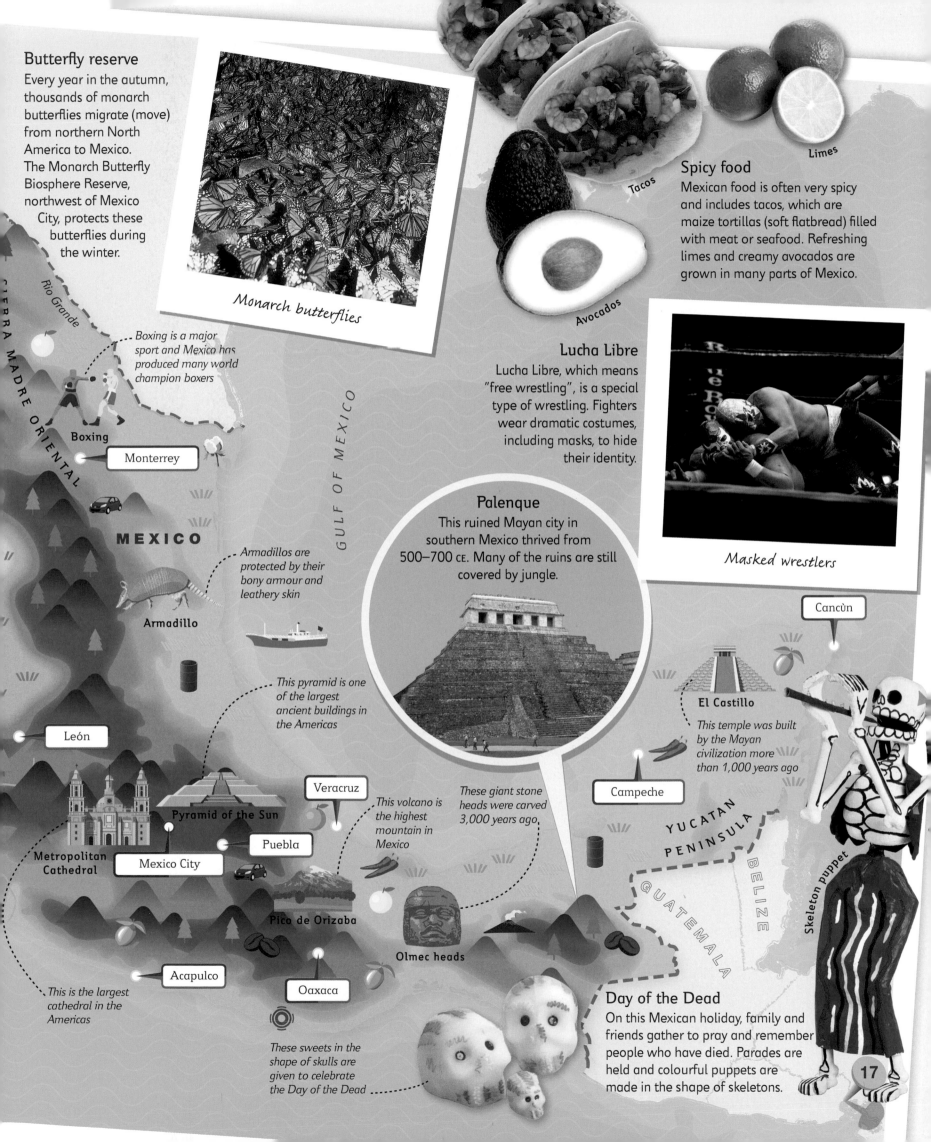

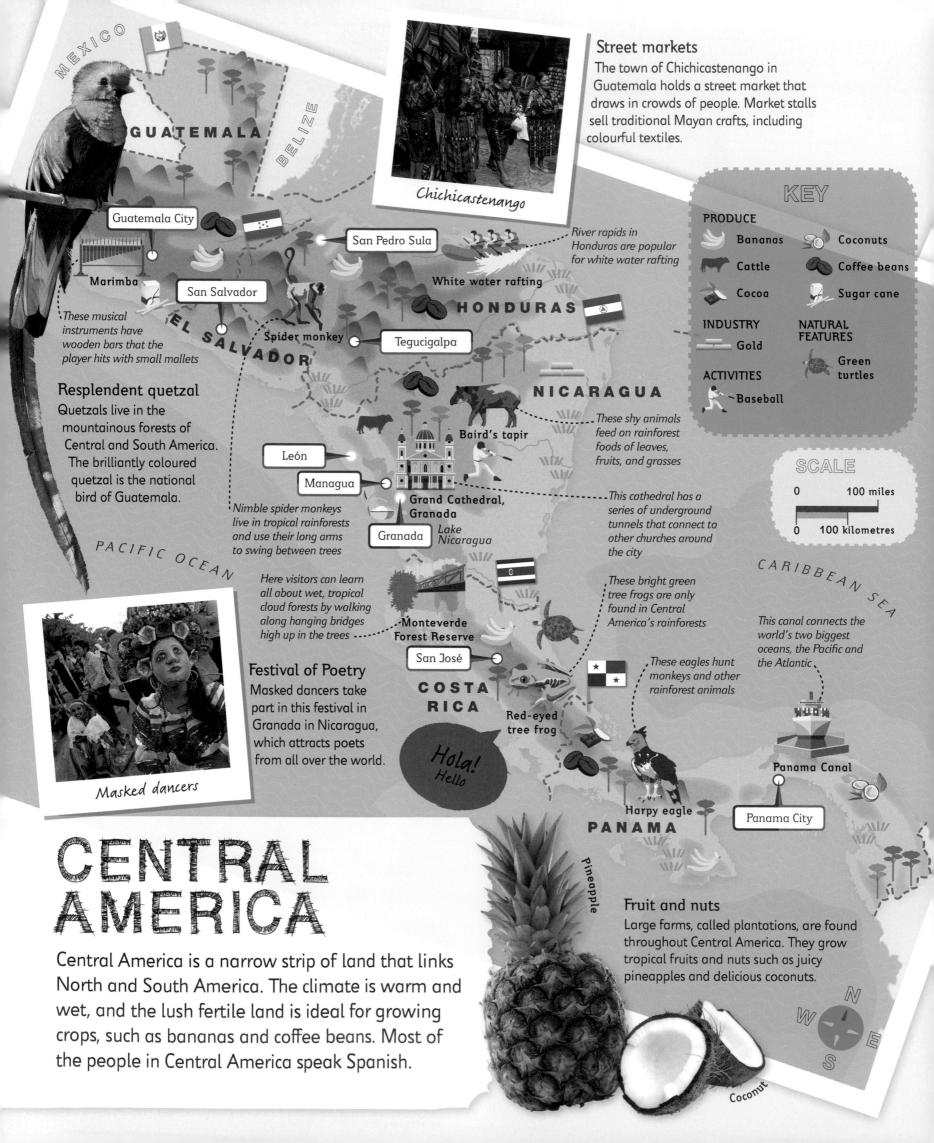

Street markets

The town of Chichicastenango in Guatemala holds a street market that draws in crowds of people. Market stalls sell traditional Mayan crafts, including colourful textiles.

Chichicastenango

KEY

PRODUCE
Bananas
Coconuts
Cattle
Coffee beans
Cocoa
Sugar cane

INDUSTRY
Gold

NATURAL FEATURES
Green turtles

ACTIVITIES
Baseball

SCALE

0 — 100 miles

0 — 100 kilometres

MEXICO

GUATEMALA

BELIZE

Guatemala City

San Pedro Sula

River rapids in Honduras are popular for white water rafting

Marimba

White water rafting

San Salvador

These musical instruments have wooden bars that the player hits with small mallets

HONDURAS

EL SALVADOR

Spider monkey

Tegucigalpa

NICARAGUA

Baird's tapir

These shy animals feed on rainforest foods of leaves, fruits, and grasses

Resplendent quetzal

Quetzals live in the mountainous forests of Central and South America. The brilliantly coloured quetzal is the national bird of Guatemala.

León

Managua

Grand Cathedral, Granada

This cathedral has a series of underground tunnels that connect to other churches around the city

Nimble spider monkeys live in tropical rainforests and use their long arms to swing between trees

Granada

Lake Nicaragua

PACIFIC OCEAN

CARIBBEAN SEA

Here visitors can learn all about wet, tropical cloud forests by walking along hanging bridges high up in the trees

These bright green tree frogs are only found in Central America's rainforests

This canal connects the world's two biggest oceans, the Pacific and the Atlantic

Monteverde Forest Reserve

San José

These eagles hunt monkeys and other rainforest animals

Festival of Poetry

Masked dancers take part in this festival in Granada in Nicaragua, which attracts poets from all over the world.

COSTA RICA

Hola! Hello

Red-eyed tree frog

Harpy eagle

PANAMA

Panama Canal

Panama City

Masked dancers

CENTRAL AMERICA

Central America is a narrow strip of land that links North and South America. The climate is warm and wet, and the lush fertile land is ideal for growing crops, such as bananas and coffee beans. Most of the people in Central America speak Spanish.

Pineapple

Fruit and nuts

Large farms, called plantations, are found throughout Central America. They grow tropical fruits and nuts such as juicy pineapples and delicious coconuts.

Coconut

N W E S

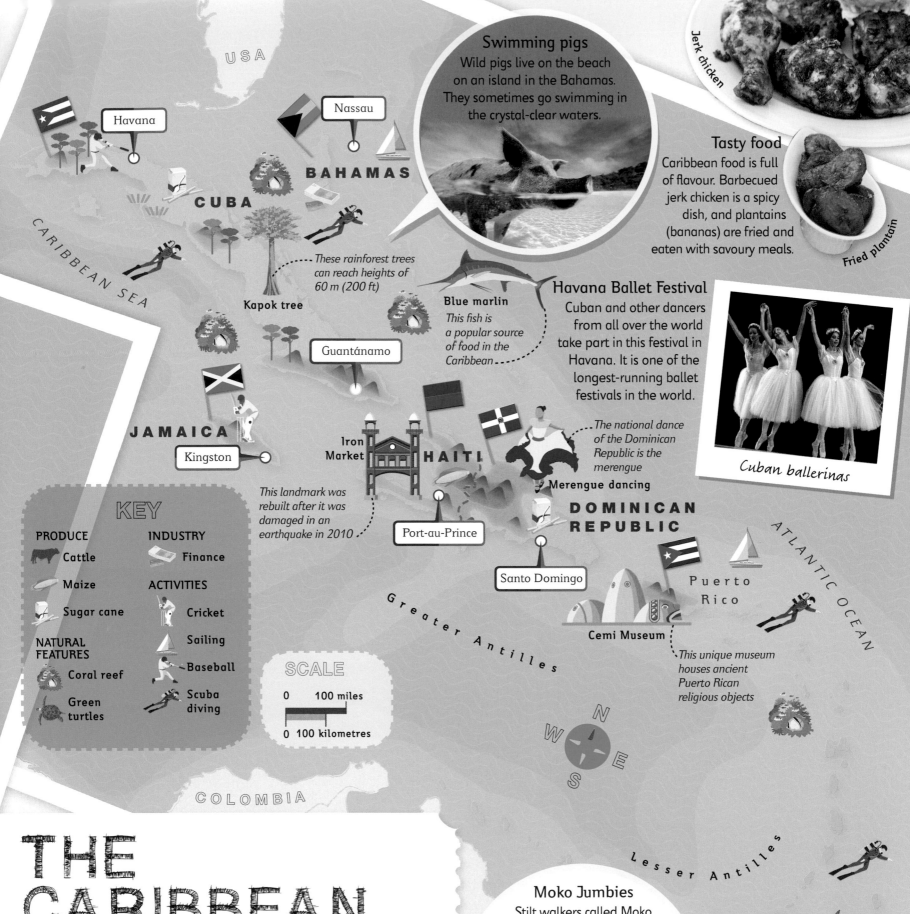

USA

Havana

Nassau

BAHAMAS

CUBA

CARIBBEAN SEA

Swimming pigs
Wild pigs live on the beach on an island in the Bahamas. They sometimes go swimming in the crystal-clear waters.

Jerk chicken

Tasty food
Caribbean food is full of flavour. Barbecued jerk chicken is a spicy dish, and plantains (bananas) are fried and eaten with savoury meals.

Fried plantain

These rainforest trees can reach heights of 60 m (200 ft)

Kapok tree

Blue marlin
This fish is a popular source of food in the Caribbean

Havana Ballet Festival
Cuban and other dancers from all over the world take part in this festival in Havana. It is one of the longest-running ballet festivals in the world.

Guantánamo

Cuban ballerinas

JAMAICA

Iron Market

HAITI

The national dance of the Dominican Republic is the merengue

Merengue dancing

Kingston

This landmark was rebuilt after it was damaged in an earthquake in 2010

Port-au-Prince

DOMINICAN REPUBLIC

Santo Domingo

ATLANTIC OCEAN

KEY

PRODUCE
Cattle
Maize
Sugar cane

NATURAL FEATURES
Coral reef
Green turtles

INDUSTRY
Finance

ACTIVITIES
Cricket
Sailing
Baseball
Scuba diving

Puerto Rico

Cemi Museum

This unique museum houses ancient Puerto Rican religious objects

Greater Antilles

SCALE
0   100 miles
0   100 kilometres

N
W   E
S

COLOMBIA

THE CARIBBEAN

Golden beaches, coral reefs, carnivals, and festivals are all part of life in the Caribbean. This group of small island nations lies between North and South America. The islands have a tropical climate and warm seas that attract thousands of tourists.

Lesser Antilles

Moko Jumbies
Stilt walkers called Moko Jumbies wear colourful costumes and dance in festivals such as the Trinidad and Tobago Carnival.

Port-of-Spain

TRINIDAD AND TOBAGO

19

CLIMATES

The weather that is typical of an area is called a climate. Climates vary around the world. The polar regions at the top and bottom of the Earth are the coldest places. Moving towards the Equator, the climate gets warmer. Different animals and plants are suited to different types of climate.

The world is getting warmer. The average temperature has risen by 1.1°C (2°F) since 1880.

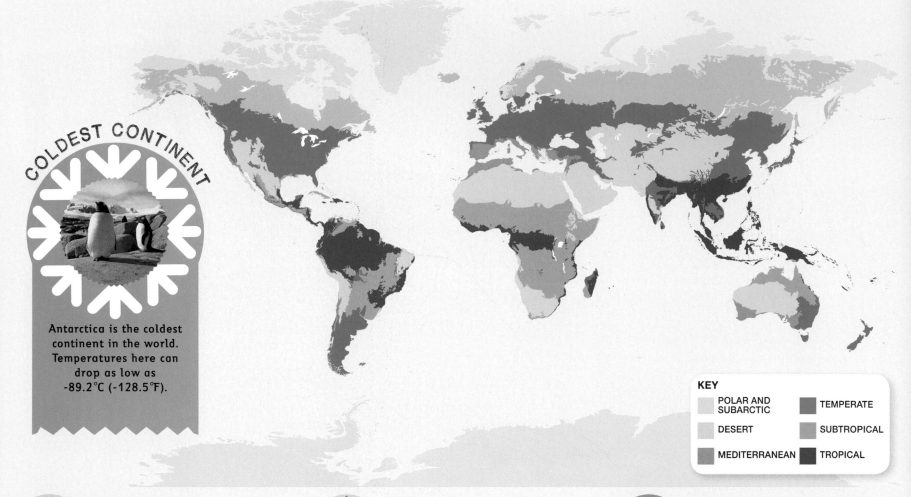

COLDEST CONTINENT

Antarctica is the coldest continent in the world. Temperatures here can drop as low as -89.2°C (-128.5°F).

KEY

POLAR AND SUBARCTIC	TEMPERATE
DESERT	SUBTROPICAL
MEDITERRANEAN	TROPICAL

POLAR AND SUBARCTIC

The climate around the North and South Poles is freezing cold and icy. Subarctic regions lie south of the North Pole, where the climate is a little warmer and some plants can survive.

DESERT

A desert climate is dry, with very little rainfall each year. Many deserts are very hot in the day and cold at night. Only a few plants and animals can survive in this harsh climate.

MEDITERRANEAN

Regions close to the Mediterranean Sea have hot, dry summers and cool, wet winters. This type of climate also describes places with similar weather patterns, such as California, USA.

TEMPERATE

Areas with a temperate climate, such as the British Isles, have warm summers and cool winters. This kind of climate suits deciduous trees, which lose their leaves in winter.

SUBTROPICAL

Hot regions of the world with dry and rainy seasons have a subtropical climate. African savannas, which are large grasslands with few trees, have this kind of climate.

TROPICAL

A tropical climate is hot and rainy. Regions with this kind of climate are near the Equator. Dense rainforests grow here. The Amazon rainforest is an example of a tropical region.

Death Valley,
California, USA
56.7°C (134°F)

Kebili,
Tunisia
55°C (131°F)

Tirat Tsvi,
Israel
54°C (129°F)

Sulaibiya, Kuwait
53.5°C (128.3°F)

Mohenjo-daro,
Pakistan
53.5°C (128.3°F)

Snag, Yukon,
Canada
-63°C (-81.4°F)

Oymyakon,
Russia
-67.7°C (-90°F)

Klinck,
Greenland
-69.6°C (-93.3°F)

South Pole,
Antarctica
-82.8°C (-117°F)

Vostok Station,
Antarctica
-89.2°C (-128.5°F)

Hot and cold places

The hottest places on Earth are in desert regions. They are hotter than tropical areas, because there are no clouds to block the Sun. The coldest places are polar regions. They get less sunlight than other places.

Five rainiest places

A state called Meghalaya in India has the world's highest rainfall each year. Here, seasonal winds called monsoons bring heavy rains. Other very wet places in the world are in rainforests or lush, hilly countryside.

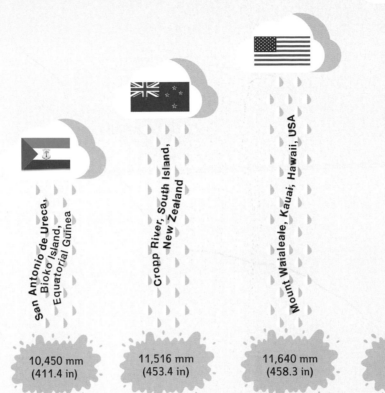

San Antonio de Ureca,
Bioko Island,
Equatorial Guinea

10,450 mm
(411.4 in)

Cropp River, South Island,
New Zealand

11,516 mm
(453.4 in)

Mount Waialeale, Kauai, Hawaii, USA

11,640 mm
(458.3 in)

Tutendo, Colombia

11,770 mm
(463.4 in)

Mawsynram, Meghalaya state, India

11,872 mm
(467.4 in)

Five driest places

Nothing grows in very dry areas because there is so little rain each year. Antarctica is the driest continent, and it is also the coldest and windiest.

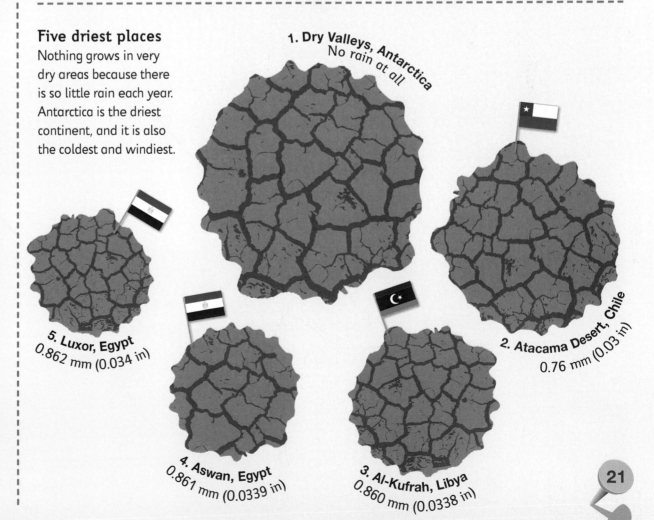

1. Dry Valleys, Antarctica
No rain at all

5. Luxor, Egypt
0.862 mm (0.034 in)

4. Aswan, Egypt
0.861 mm (0.0339 in)

3. Al-Kufrah, Libya
0.860 mm (0.0338 in)

2. Atacama Desert, Chile
0.76 mm (0.03 in)

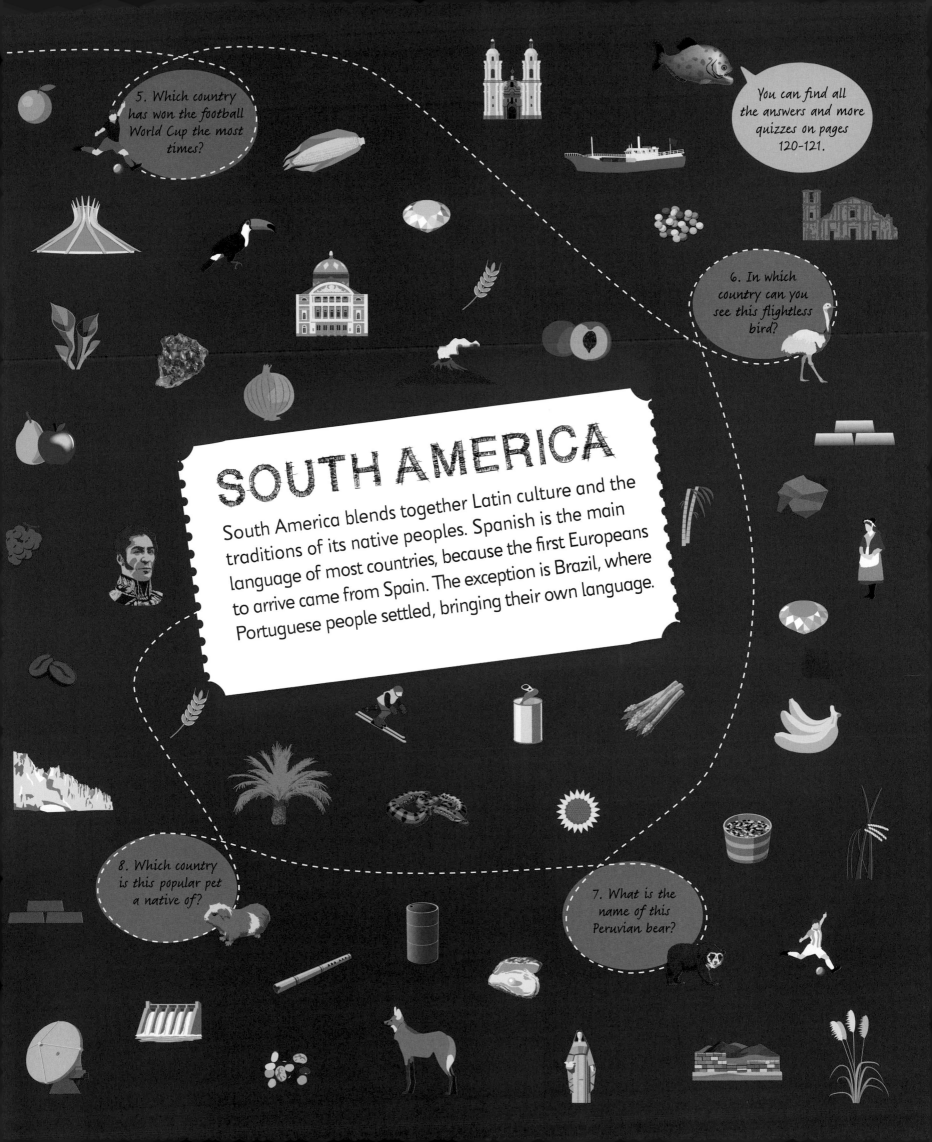

SOUTH AMERICA

South America stretches from the tropical Caribbean Sea in the north to the icy Southern Ocean in the south. The world's largest forest, the Amazon rainforest, covers most of Brazil and the northern part of the continent.

GALÁPAGOS ISLANDS (ECUADOR)

CARIBBEAN SEA

VENEZUELA

COLOMBIA

ECUADOR

PERU

BOLIVIA

PACIFIC OCEAN

CHILE

ARGENTINA

DRAKE PASSAGE

Lake Titicaca

This deep lake, high up in the Andes mountains, sits on the border between Bolivia and Peru. There are several inhabited islands on the lake, including some floating, man-made islands, built from reeds. The way of life here has changed little over the centuries.

Andes mountains

This mountain range runs like a spine down the west side of South America. It is the world's longest mountain range, stretching from the north of Colombia to the southern tip of Chile.

Amazon river

This giant river flows through the Amazon rainforest, out into the Atlantic Ocean. It carries more water than any other river in the world.

ATLANTIC OCEAN

GUYANA

SURINAME

FRENCH GUIANA (FRANCE)

BRAZIL

PARAGUAY

URUGUAY

FALKLAND ISLANDS (UNITED KINGDOM)

SCOTIA SEA

N
W E
S

São Paulo

More people live in São Paulo than in any other city in South America. It started as a tiny, isolated village, which was founded by Portuguese settlers in the 16th century. After gold was discovered nearby in the 1690s, it began to grow and this bustling city is now Brazil's main business centre.

SCALE

0   500 miles   1000 miles

0   1000 kilometres

Pampas

This vast, grassy plain stretches over the eastern part of Argentina, most of Uruguay and the extreme south of Brazil. Parts are now farmed and huge quantities of wheat and vegetables grow here. The grasslands are perfect for rearing animals, including sheep and cattle. Argentine beef is some of the best in the world.

COLOMBIA AND VENEZUELA

Colombia and Venezuela lie in the northwest corner of South America. To the north of these countries is the Caribbean Sea and to the south the Amazon rainforest. These Spanish-speaking countries are rich in emeralds, diamonds, and gold.

Scarlet macaw
This large, noisy parrot lives in the rainforests of both Colombia and Venezuela. It eats nuts, seeds, and fruit.

Angel Falls
The Angel Falls is the world's highest waterfall. Water plunges 979 m (3,212 ft) into the rainforest.

CARIBBEAN SEA

N W E S

PANAMA

PACIFIC OCEAN

ECUADOR

PERU

Bolívar helped several South American countries, including his home country of Venezuela, gain independence

Caracas

Valencia

Maracaibo

Simón Bolívar

Barranquilla

Lake Maracaibo

This huge statue of the Virgin Mary symbolizes world peace

Virgen de la Paz

Cuidad Bolívar

Apure

Orinoco

VENEZUELA

San Cristóbal

Giant anteater

Cauca

Magdalena

Medellín

Anteaters feed on ants and termites, lapping them up with their long, sticky tongue

Puerto Ayacucho

Caura

GUYANA

Bogotá

Meta

Insects that land on this plant are trapped and eaten

Pitcher plant

This cathedral sits in a square in the centre of Bogotá

Bogotá Cathedral

Puerto Inírida

BRAZIL

Santiago de Cali

Guaviare

Tumaco

COLOMBIA

Mitú

Hola! Hello

KEY

Pasto

This snake can swallow a deer whole

Anaconda

Caquetá

SCALE
0 — 200 miles
0 — 200 kilometres

San Agustín Park
This park is home to the largest group of ancient religious monuments in South America. Some of them are nearly 2,000 years old.

PRODUCE
- Bananas
- Coffee
- Cut flowers
- Rice
- Sugar cane
- Maize

ACTIVITIES
- Baseball

NATURAL FEATURES
- Earthquakes
- Volcanoes

INDUSTRY
- Oil
- Gas
- Nickel
- Diamonds
- Pearls
- Gold
- Emeralds
- Iron ore
- Palm oil

Pre-Columbian statue

PERU

Peru has some stunning scenery, ranging from dense rainforest to snow-capped peaks. The Andes mountain range runs the length of the country and is a popular destination for hiking. Peru is known for its brightly coloured, traditional textiles and its delicious fish and potato dishes.

San Pedro market

Craft market
The native Quechua people live on traditional farms high up in the Andes. Cusco's San Pedro market sells colourful Quechua textiles.

Adiós! Goodbye

This large-winged bird lives in the Andes mountains

Andean condor

Chiclayo

Trujillo

Some structures at this site are nearly 3,000 years old

Chavin archaeological site

Lima

This magnificent monastery was built by the Spanish

Monastery of San Francisco

Potatoes
Potatoes are native to Peru. Over 4,000 varieties grow here and come in many different sizes, shapes, and colours, including pink, purple, orange, and yellow ones.

Llamas are kept for their meat, wool, and carrying loads

Llama

Arequipa

Iquitos

Yurimaguas

The tarka is a traditional Andean wooden flute

Pucallpa

Flute

Guinea pig

This native of Peru is now a popular pet worldwide

The cream fur around this bear's eyes make it look like it is wearing glasses

Spectacled bear

Amazon

Urubamba

Emperor tamarin
This monkey lives in the Amazon rainforest. Both male and female adults have a long, white moustache.

Machu Picchu
Machu Picchu is an ancient Inca city in the Andes. Its ruins are one of the world's most popular tourist attractions.

Boats made from dried reeds are used for fishing

Cusco

Lake Titicaca

Reed boats

COLOMBIA

ECUADOR

BRAZIL

PERU

PACIFIC OCEAN

ANDES

BOLIVIA

CHILE

KEY

PRODUCE
- Asparagus
- Coffee
- Sugarcane
- Quinoa

INDUSTRY
- Fishing
- Timber
- Gold
- Silver
- Copper
- Cotton
- Iron ore

ACTIVITIES
- Hiking

NATURAL FEATURES
- Earthquakes

SCALE
0 — 200 miles

0 — 200 kilometres

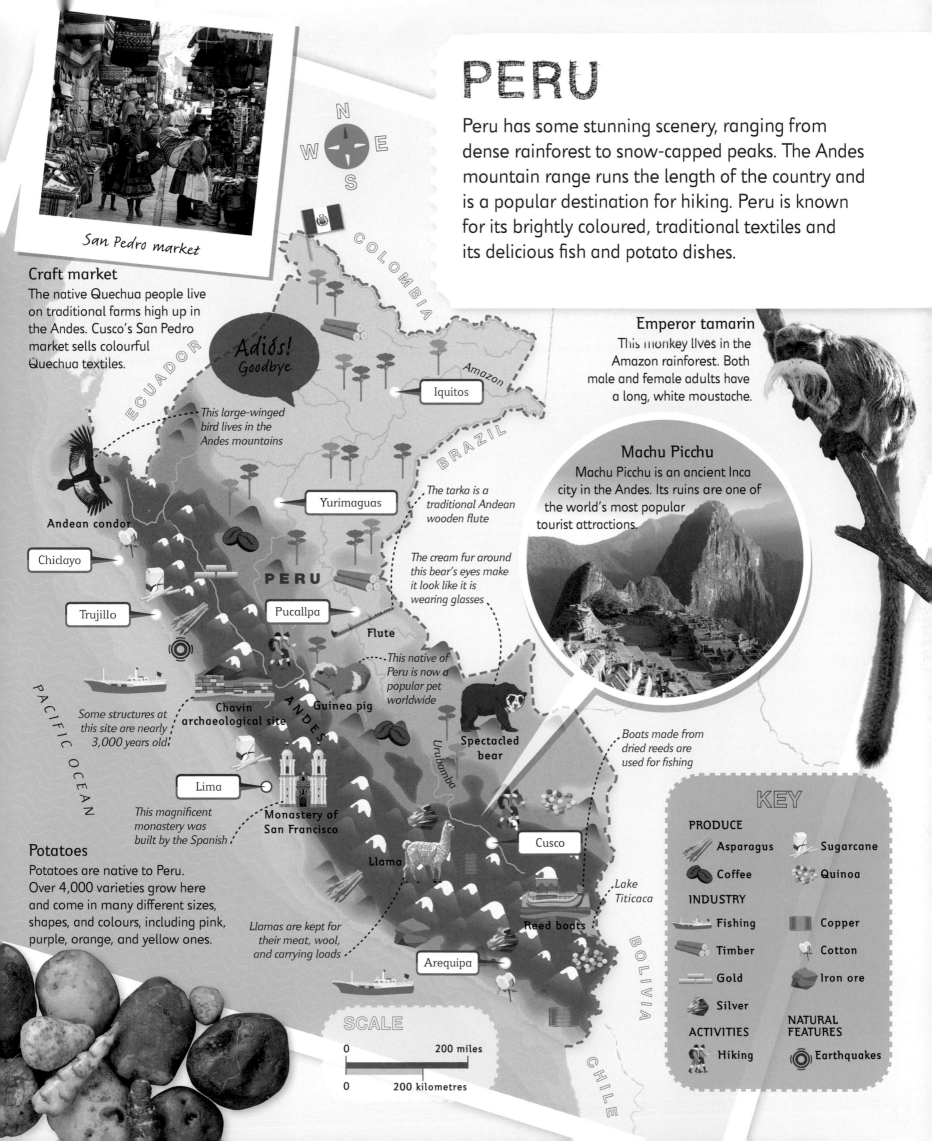

BRAZIL

Brazil is the largest country in South America and has a great variety of people and cultures. Most Brazilians live in big, crowded cities and speak Portuguese, the country's official language, while more than 200 tribal groups have their own unique languages.

Coffee and oranges

Brazil is the world's largest producer of oranges and coffee beans. About 75 per cent of the orange crop is turned into juice and exported. There are about 300,000 coffee farms across the country and Brazilians drink half of the coffee they produce.

Coffee beans

Oranges

Rainforest people

People have lived in the Amazon rainforest for thousands of years. The Yanomami are one of the largest tribes. They live in large, circular huts with palm leaf roofs.

Rainforest life

The vast Amazon rainforest is packed with plant and animal life. An amazing number of insect species live there – about 2.5 million!

The bright blue upper wings help these large butterflies to see each other in the dark forest

Morpho butterfly

Some people use canoes to travel along the Amazon. Larger boats are used for tourists and trade

Canoes

SCALE

0   200 miles   400 miles

0   400 kilometres

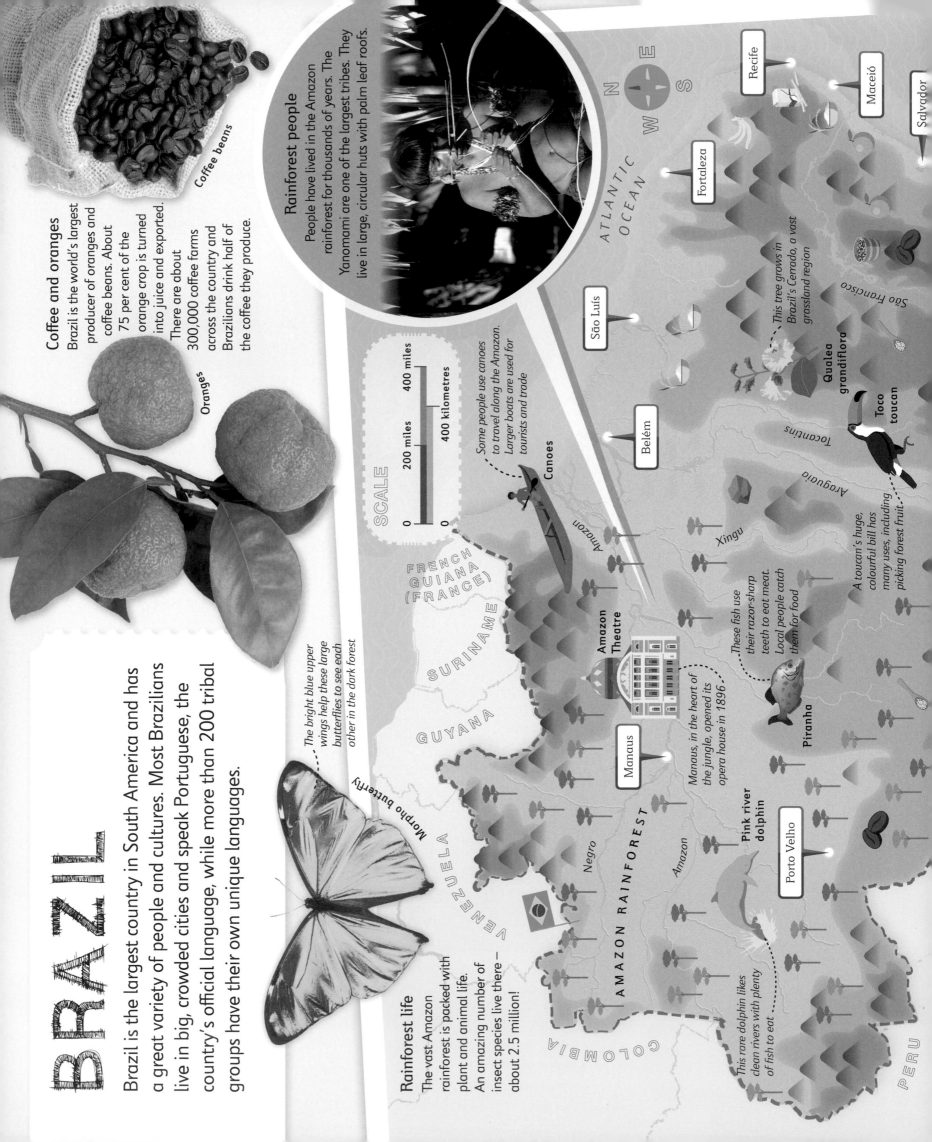

ATLANTIC OCEAN

N W S E

Recife

Maceió

Salvador

Fortaleza

São Luís

Belém

This tree grows in Brazil's Cerrado, a vast grassland region

Qualea grandiflora

Toco toucan

São Francisco

A toucan's huge, colourful bill has many uses, including picking forest fruit

Tocantins

Araguaia

Xingu

Amazon

FRENCH GUIANA (FRANCE)

SURINAME

GUYANA

Amazon Theatre

Manaus, in the heart of the jungle, opened its opera house in 1896

These fish use their razor-sharp teeth to eat meat. Local people catch them for food

Piranha

Manaus

VENEZUELA

Negro

Amazon

AMAZON RAINFOREST

Pink river dolphin

This rare dolphin likes clean rivers with plenty of fish to eat

Porto Velho

COLOMBIA

PERU

Brasília replaced Rio as the capital in 1960. The modern cathedral looks like a crown of thorns

Belo Horizonte

Christ the Redeemer
This giant statue overlooks the city and is one of Rio's main landmarks

Rio de Janeiro

Sugar Loaf Mountain
This domed mountain rises above Rio. Stunning views of the city can be enjoyed by people who take a cable car to the top. Rio was chosen to host the Summer Olympics in 2016.

Cathedral

Brasília

Goiânia

São Paulo

Curitiba

Porto Alegre

Olá!
Hello

São Miguel Mission

Built in 1687, this Catholic church is now a ruin

Lagoa dos Patos

Capybara

PANTANAL

This rodent is as big as a large dog and lives in marshy areas like the Pantanal

Paraná

BOLIVIA

PARAGUAY

URUGUAY

ARGENTINA

Every jaguar has a unique pattern of spots on its coat

Jaguar
This big cat lives in the Amazon rainforest. Jaguars are strong swimmers and they have a powerful bite.

Capoeira
This martial art involves music, dance, and acrobatics. Capoeira was developed in Brazil 500 years ago by people from West Africa and is a fun form of exercise.

Acrobatic moves

Football
Brazilians love football. The country has won the football World Cup more times (five) than any other country. Many famous footballers come from Brazil, including Pelé, one of the greatest players of all time.

Football on the beach

Iguaçu Falls
This spectacular series of waterfalls stretches across the border between Brazil and Argentina. The forests surrounding the falls are protected by two national parks.

KEY

RESOURCES
- Gold
- Iron
- Diamonds
- Oil
- Hydroelectric power

ACTIVITIES
- Football

PRODUCE
- Coffee
- Oranges
- Bananas
- Soya beans
- Dried beans
- Sugar cane
- Rice

ARGENTINA AND CHILE

These two countries stretch across the southern part of South America. Between them lies the Andes mountains. Argentina's dramatic landscape includes the rugged hills of Patagonia, while Chile is a long, thin country with both desert and fertile farmland.

Argentine tango
This Latin American style of dance originated in Buenos Aires. Dancers hold one another close and walk together in time to the music, with one partner taking the lead.

Tango dancers

Highest vineyard
The highest vineyard in the world lies at 3,111 m (10,200 ft) in the Calchaquí Valley in northern Argentina.

Atacama Desert
The Atacama Desert is one of the driest places on Earth. This strip of land between the Pacific Ocean and the Andes mountains receives little rainfall, because the mountains block the rain.

Fertile land
The land of Central Chile is rich and fertile. Here, fruits, such as juicy peaches, are grown in orchards. Grapes also flourish, and Chilean wine is exported all over the world.

Maned wolves look like a small wolf or a large red fox, but are a different species, unique to the grasslands of South America

This mine is one of the largest open-cast (surface) copper mines in the world

One of the world's most powerful observatories, which captures images of objects in outer space, is based in the Atacama Desert

Salt lakes and other deposits formed in the Atacama Desert when lakes dried out

The snowy slopes of the Andes are perfect for skiing

Tall species of flowering grass grow in the lowland grasslands of the Pampas

The successful Argentinian football team has a big rivalry with neighbouring Brazil

Rodeo is Chile's national sport – pairs of riders known as "Huasos" work together to round up cattle

PERU

BOLIVIA

PARAGUAY

BRAZIL

URUGUAY

CHILE

ARGENTINA

Bermejo

Parand

Uruguay

Loa

Maipo

ATACAMA DESERT

ANDES

Aconcagua

Chiquicamata copper mine

ALMA space observatory

Salt lakes

Maned wolf

San Miguel de Tucumán

Salta

Pampas grass

Football

Córdoba

Rosario

Mendoza

Santiago

Valparaíso

Skiing

Huaso rodeo

Antofagasta

PACIFIC OCEAN

This museum in Buenos Aires features many spectacular art exhibits

Buenos Aires

Río de la Plata

MALBA Museum of Modern Art

Polo

Beef steak and sauce

Argentina is well known for producing top-quality beef. Chimichurri sauce, made from fresh herbs, garlic, and olive oil, is often served with steak.

KEY

PRODUCE

Vineyards
Onions
Maize
Beef cattle
Sunflowers
Peaches
Soya beans
Sheep
Apples and pears
Wheat

INDUSTRY

Hydroelectric power
Copper
Timber
Zinc
Lead
Iron
Fishing
Oil
Tin

NATURAL FEATURES

Volcanoes
Earthquakes

Polo players compete in teams on horseback to score goals against each other by hitting a ball with a mallet

This large, flightless bird hunts for reptiles and insects in the grasslands

Rhea

ATLANTIC OCEAN

P A M P A S

N
W E
S

Welsh people settled in the remote region of Patagonia in the 1800s. They speak their own special dialect of Welsh.

P A T A G O N I A

Patagonian Welsh

Hola!
Hello

A N D E S

Ice flows into Lake Argentino from the Perito Moreno Glacier

This is one of seven species of penguin that live in South America

Gaucho herding cattle

Cattle herding

Beef cattle is an important industry on the flat, treeless plains of the Pampas. Argentine cowboys, known as "gauchos", herd the cattle on huge ranches.

Lake Argentino

Perito Moreno Glacier

Magellanic penguins

Punta Arenas

Talcahuano

Bío Bío

Maule

SCALE

0   200 miles
0   200 kilometres

Stone heads

Easter Island

This Chilean island lies in the Pacific Ocean, 3,686 km (2,290 miles) west of the mainland. It is known for its huge stone statues, called moai, that were carved by local people hundreds of years ago.

Alpacas

Alpacas are kept in herds high in the mountains of northern Chile. Their thick hair can be woven to make blankets, hats, and sweaters.

POPULATION

The number of people living in the world is growing fast. In 1800, the world's population was about 1 billion. Today, there are more than 7.8 billion people worldwide. More than half of these people live in cities, rather than in the countryside. The population is growing because of healthier eating and better health care, which means that people are living longer.

Emptiest country

The emptiest country in the world is Mongolia, with on average of about two people for every square kilometre of land (about five people per square mile).

MONGOLIA

Most populated countries

These five countries have some of the biggest populations in the world. They are all large countries with plenty of farmland for growing crops.

1. CHINA
1.44 billion people

2. INDIA
1.38 billion people

3. USA
331 million people

4. INDONESIA
273 million people

5. BRAZIL
212 million people

Who lives where?

This chart shows the percentage of the world's population in each continent. Asia is by far the world's most populated continent.

ASIA
60%

32

Most populated cities

The biggest city in most countries is usually, but not always, its capital city. A huge, sprawling city is also known as a metropolis. This chart shows the most populated city in each continent.

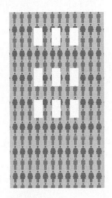

The Greater Tokyo area has nearly the same population as the whole of Canada!

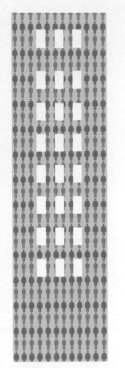

Tokyo, Japan, Asia
37 million people

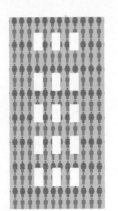

Mexico City, Mexico, North America
22 million people

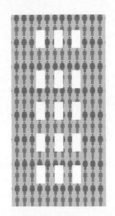

São Paulo, Brazil, South America
22 million people

Cairo, Egypt, Africa
21 million people

Moscow, Russia, Europe
12 million people

Melbourne, Australia, Australasia
5 million people

City versus countryside

In many parts of the world, cities are growing fast. People are moving, or migrating, from rural areas (the countryside) into towns and cities. Worldwide, about 54 per cent of people live in cities and about 46 per cent live in the countryside.

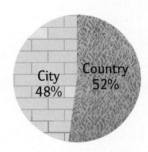

City 48% Country 52%

ASIA

Country 29% City 71%

AUSTRALASIA

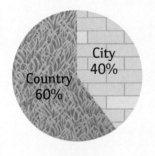

Country 60% City 40%

AFRICA

Country 17% City 83%

SOUTH AMERICA

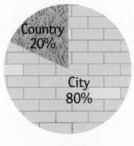

Country 20% City 80%

NORTH AMERICA

Country 26% City 74%

EUROPE

LARGEST CHILD POPULATION

India is the country with the most children. It has about 450 million children. This is about 40 per cent of India's population.

AFRICA 16%

NORTH AMERICA 8%

AUSTRALASIA 1%

EUROPE 10%

SOUTH AMERICA 5%

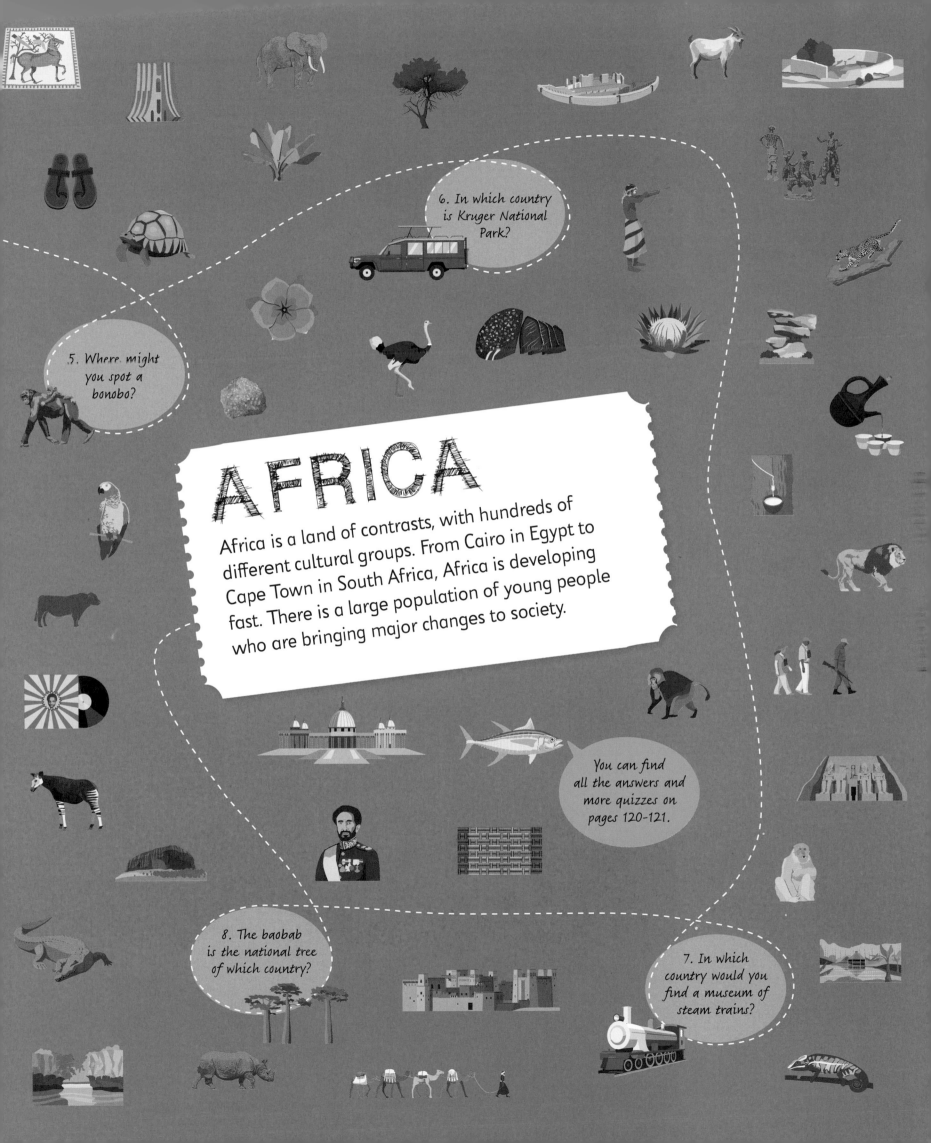

AFRICA

Africa is a land of contrasts, with hundreds of different cultural groups. From Cairo in Egypt to Cape Town in South Africa, Africa is developing fast. There is a large population of young people who are bringing major changes to society.

5. Where might you spot a bonobo?

6. In which country is Kruger National Park?

7. In which country would you find a museum of steam trains?

8. The baobab is the national tree of which country?

You can find all the answers and more quizzes on pages 120-121.

AFRICA

Africa is the world's second largest continent. The dry countries bordering the Mediterranean Sea in the north are cut off from the rest of Africa by the Sahara Desert. South of the Sahara are grassy plains and dense tropical rainforests, where many unique wild animals live.

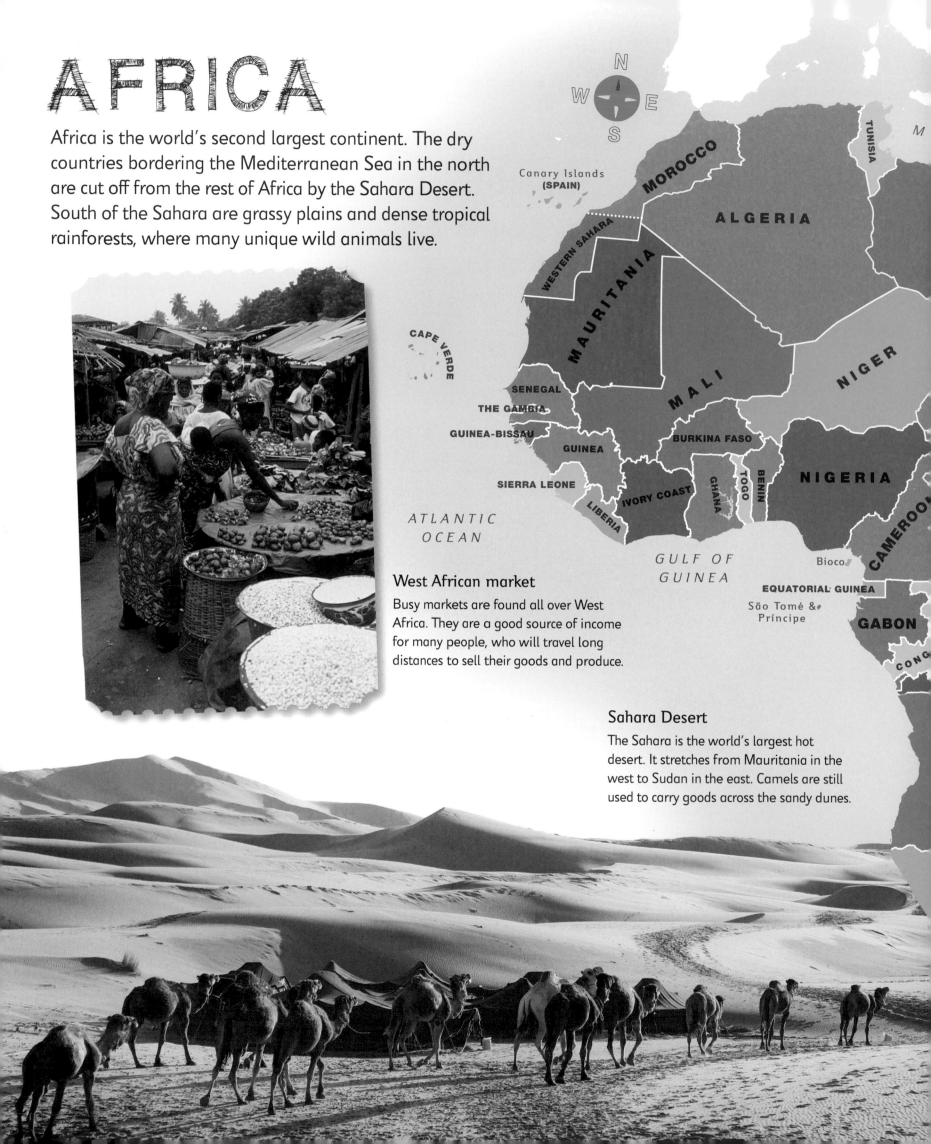

N W E S

Canary Islands
(SPAIN)

MOROCCO

TUNISIA

M

ALGERIA

WESTERN SAHARA

MAURITANIA

CAPE VERDE

MALI

NIGER

SENEGAL

THE GAMBIA

GUINEA-BISSAU

GUINEA

BURKINA FASO

NIGERIA

SIERRA LEONE

IVORY COAST

GHANA

TOGO

BENIN

ATLANTIC
OCEAN

LIBERIA

GULF OF
GUINEA

Bioco

CAMEROON

EQUATORIAL GUINEA

São Tomé &
Príncipe

GABON

CONG

West African market

Busy markets are found all over West Africa. They are a good source of income for many people, who will travel long distances to sell their goods and produce.

Sahara Desert

The Sahara is the world's largest hot desert. It stretches from Mauritania in the west to Sudan in the east. Camels are still used to carry goods across the sandy dunes.

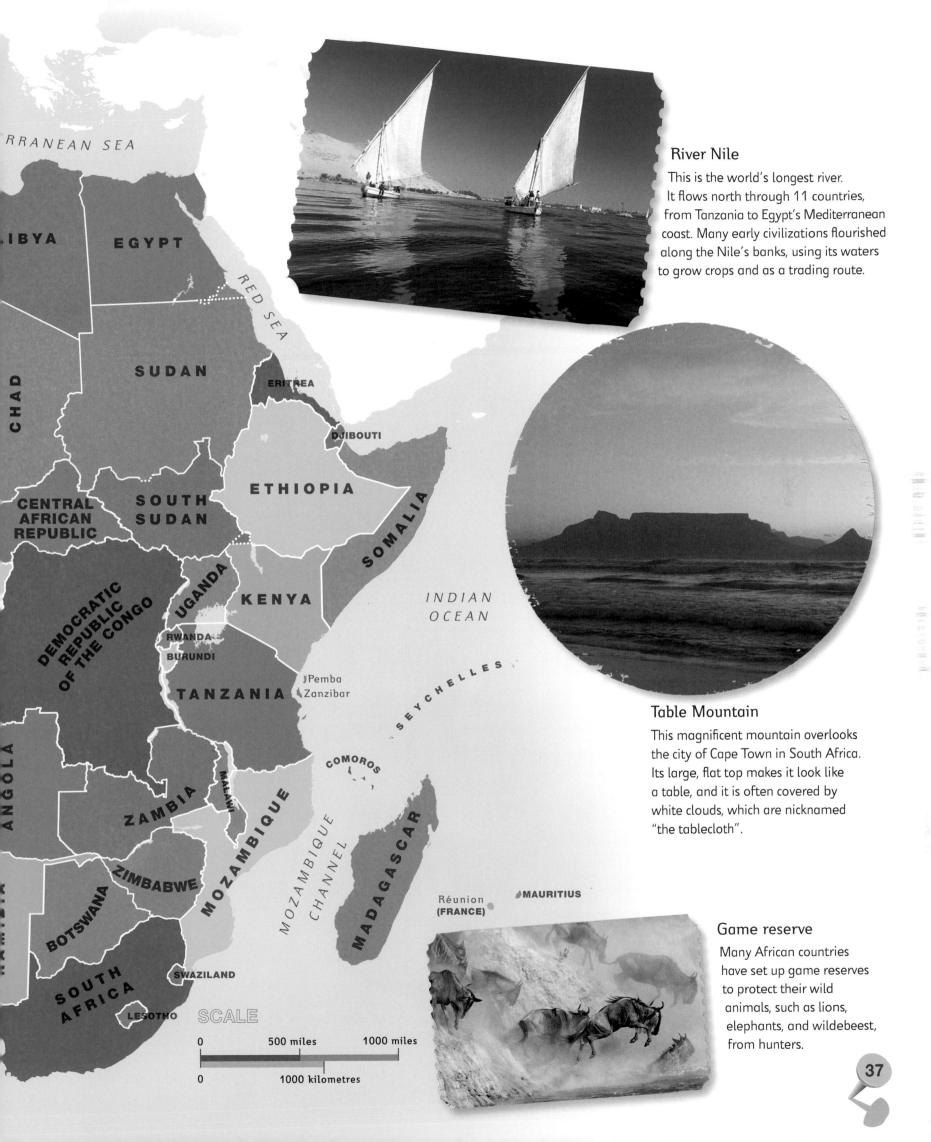

MEDITERRANEAN SEA

RED SEA

LIBYA

EGYPT

CHAD

SUDAN

ERITREA

DJIBOUTI

CENTRAL
AFRICAN
REPUBLIC

SOUTH
SUDAN

ETHIOPIA

SOMALIA

DEMOCRATIC
REPUBLIC
OF THE CONGO

UGANDA

KENYA

RWANDA

BURUNDI

INDIAN
OCEAN

ANGOLA

TANZANIA

Pemba
Zanzibar

SEYCHELLES

ZAMBIA

MALAWI

COMOROS

ZIMBABWE

MOZAMBIQUE

MOZAMBIQUE
CHANNEL

MADAGASCAR

Réunion
(FRANCE)

MAURITIUS

BOTSWANA

SWAZILAND

SOUTH
AFRICA

LESOTHO

SCALE

0   500 miles   1000 miles

0   1000 kilometres

River Nile

This is the world's longest river. It flows north through 11 countries, from Tanzania to Egypt's Mediterranean coast. Many early civilizations flourished along the Nile's banks, using its waters to grow crops and as a trading route.

Table Mountain

This magnificent mountain overlooks the city of Cape Town in South Africa. Its large, flat top makes it look like a table, and it is often covered by white clouds, which are nicknamed "the tablecloth".

Game reserve

Many African countries have set up game reserves to protect their wild animals, such as lions, elephants, and wildebeest, from hunters.

NORTH AFRICA

The four countries of Morocco, Algeria, Tunisia, and Libya sit side by side at the northern end of Africa. Towns and cities are dotted along the Mediterranean coast, where lively markets are found alongside ancient ruins. Vast areas of North Africa are sandy desert, with rich oil reserves in some places.

SPAIN

Tangier

Markets all over Morocco sell traditional leather goods

Rabat

Casablanca

Fès

Leather goods

Meknès

Marrakesh

Aït Benhaddou

ATLAS MOUNTAINS

Barbary macaque

Béchar

These monkeys mainly live in the Atlas Mountains

This ancient fortified town is built from red clay

MOROCCO

ATLANTIC OCEAN

These small, venomous snakes live in the deserts of North Africa

Horned viper

Salam!
Hello

Laâyoune

Tindouf

SCALE
0 — 200 miles
0 — 200 kilometres

Western Sahara

Medina
Many North African cities have ancient walled areas, with maze-like narrow alleyways, called medinas. The Marrakesh medina contains Morocco's largest traditional market.

SAHARA DESERT

The Tuareg are a desert people, who traditionally wear blue robes

MALI

MAURITANIA

Hassan II Mosque
This huge mosque stands on the edge of the city of Casablanca in Morocco. More than 100,000 worshippers can gather here for prayer. Its 210-m (689-ft) minaret tower is the tallest in the world.

North African cuisine
Tagine, a type of stew usually made with lamb, is eaten in many parts of North Africa. Refreshing mint tea is the most popular drink.

Tuareg blue robes

Mint tea

Mint leaves

Tagine

Striped hyena
These hyenas are found throughout North Africa. They live in caves or dig dens, coming out to search for food at night.

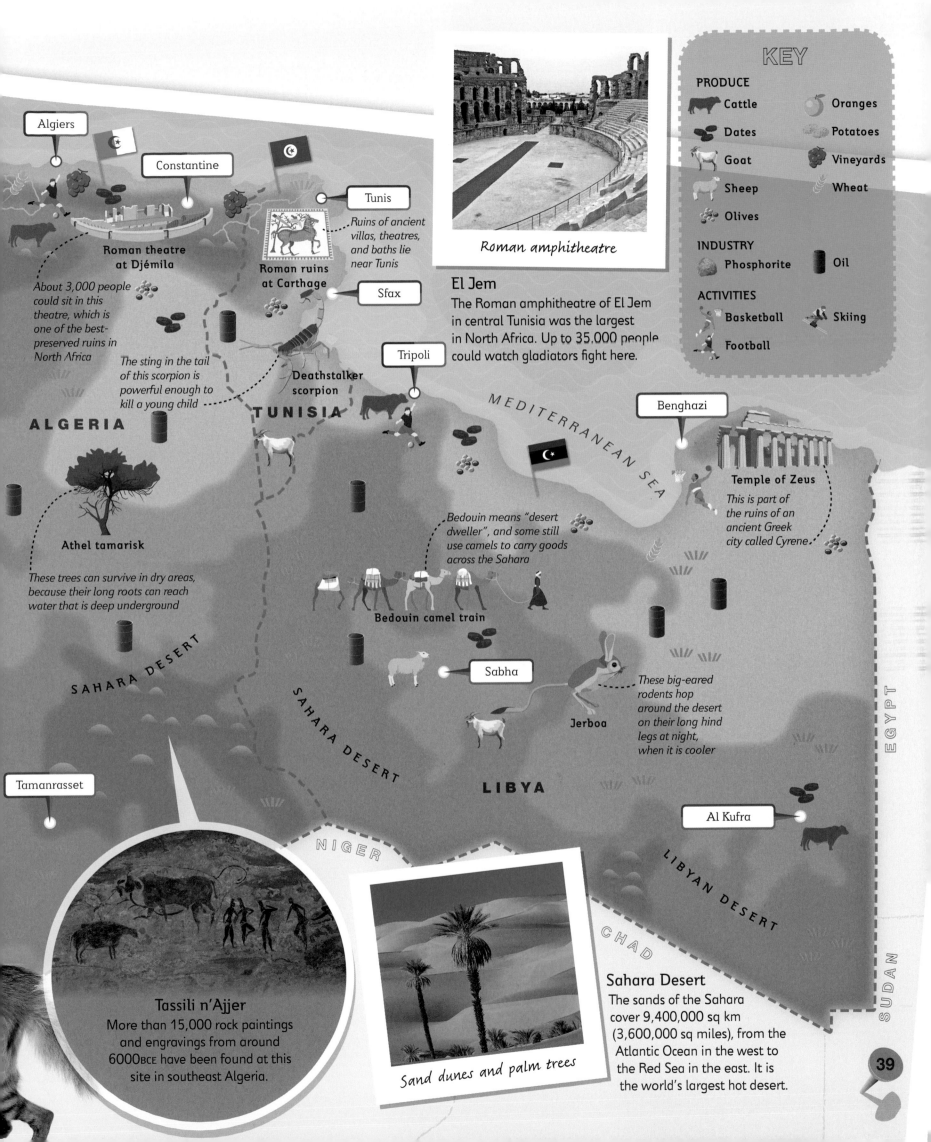

Algiers

Constantine

Tunis

Roman theatre at Djémila

About 3,000 people could sit in this theatre, which is one of the best-preserved ruins in North Africa

Roman ruins at Carthage

Ruins of ancient villas, theatres, and baths lie near Tunis

Sfax

The sting in the tail of this scorpion is powerful enough to kill a young child

Deathstalker scorpion

Tripoli

ALGERIA

TUNISIA

Athel tamarisk

These trees can survive in dry areas, because their long roots can reach water that is deep underground

SAHARA DESERT

Tamanrasset

SAHARA DESERT

Bedouin means "desert dweller", and some still use camels to carry goods across the Sahara

Bedouin camel train

Sabha

Jerboa

These big-eared rodents hop around the desert on their long hind legs at night, when it is cooler

LIBYA

Benghazi

Temple of Zeus

This is part of the ruins of an ancient Greek city called Cyrene

M E D I T E R R A N E A N   S E A

Roman amphitheatre

El Jem

The Roman amphitheatre of El Jem in central Tunisia was the largest in North Africa. Up to 35,000 people could watch gladiators fight here.

KEY

PRODUCE

- Cattle
- Oranges
- Dates
- Potatoes
- Goat
- Vineyards
- Sheep
- Wheat
- Olives

INDUSTRY

- Phosphorite
- Oil

ACTIVITIES

- Basketball
- Skiing
- Football

Al Kufra

NIGER

CHAD

LIBYAN DESERT

EGYPT

SUDAN

Tassili n'Ajjer

More than 15,000 rock paintings and engravings from around 6000BCE have been found at this site in southeast Algeria.

Sand dunes and palm trees

Sahara Desert

The sands of the Sahara cover 9,400,000 sq km (3,600,000 sq miles), from the Atlantic Ocean in the west to the Red Sea in the east. It is the world's largest hot desert.

39

EGYPT

Much of Egypt is made up of dry, sandy desert, and so most people live along the banks of the Nile River. This very long river is a vital source of water for drinking and farming. Thousands of years ago, pharaohs (kings) built pyramids along the Nile, some of which are still standing.

Mummy case
Ancient Egyptians preserved, or mummified, bodies. The specially treated body was wrapped in bandages and the mummy was then placed in a decorated case.

KEY

PRODUCE	INDUSTRY
Rice	Oil
Wheat	Fishing
Oranges	**ACTIVITIES**
Dates	Scuba diving
Cotton	**NATURAL FEATURES**
	Coral reef

Pyramids
These massive structures were built as tombs for the bodies of dead Egyptian kings and queens. The three most famous pyramids are at Giza.

SCALE

0   100 miles   200 miles

0   200 kilometres

MEDITERRANEAN SEA

This huge sandstone statue has a lion's body and a human head

Port Said

Alexandria

Suez

Cairo

Giza

Great Sphinx

SINAI PENINSULA

GULF OF SUEZ

N W E S

LIBYA

WESTERN DESERT

Large crocodiles live in the Nile, eating all kinds of animals, from fish to cattle

Nile crocodile

EGYPT

EASTERN DESERT

RED SEA

SAUDI ARABIA

Rescued ruins
When the Aswan Dam was built, it created a large reservoir called Lake Nasser. Two ancient temples had to be moved from the area that was flooded.

Some pharaohs were buried in tombs in the Valley of the Kings near Luxor

Nile

Valley of the Kings

Luxor

Salam!
Hello

This snake is one of the most venomous in Africa. One bite can kill a human in minutes

These two huge temples were important places of worship in Ancient Egypt

Feluccas are traditional wooden sailing boats, still used along the Nile

Aswan Dam

This dam opened in 1970; it generates hydroelectricity and controls flood water

Lake Nasser

Cotton tunic

Egyptian cobra

Great Temples at Abu Simbel

Felucca

SUDAN

Cotton
Cool and comfortable cotton tunics are a common form of dress in this hot country. Egyptian cotton is known for its high quality.

Camels
Camels are still used for transport in Egypt, because they can survive in very dry conditions and so can travel long distances across the desert.

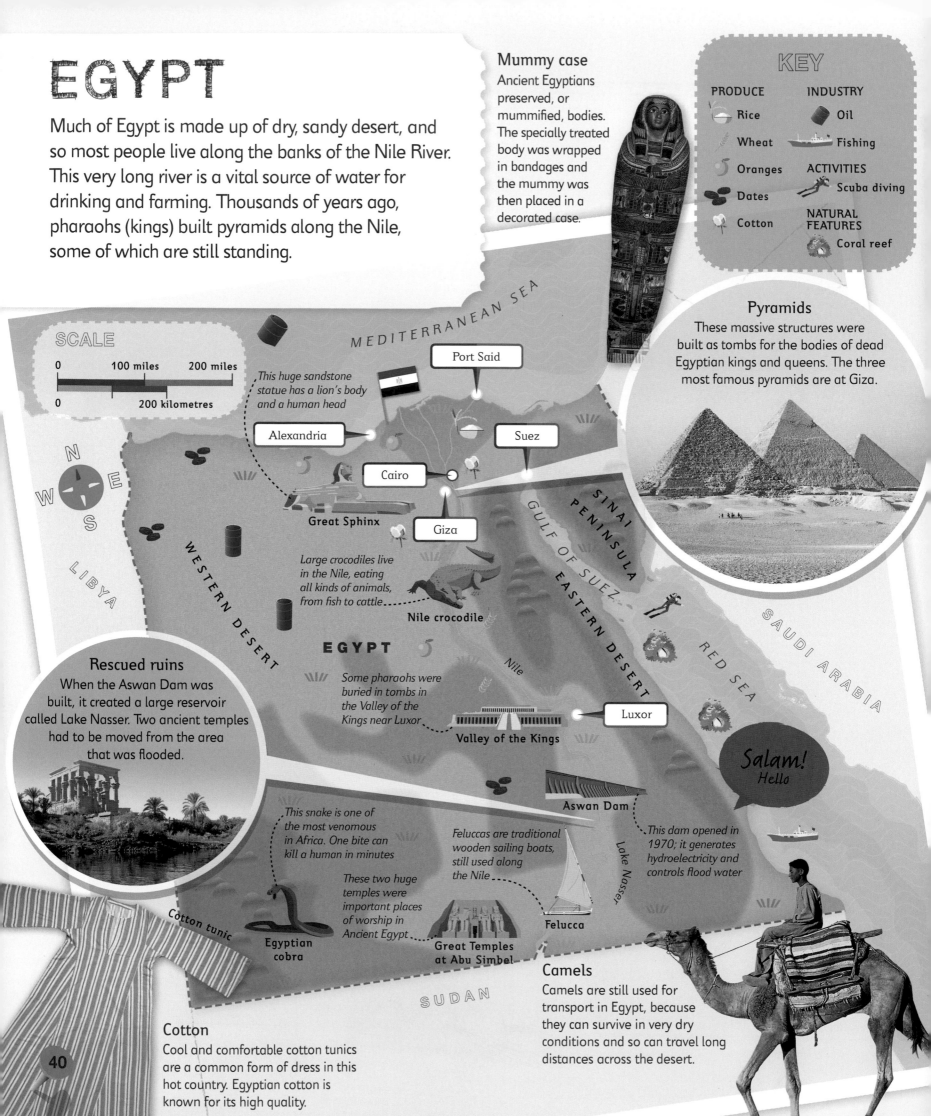

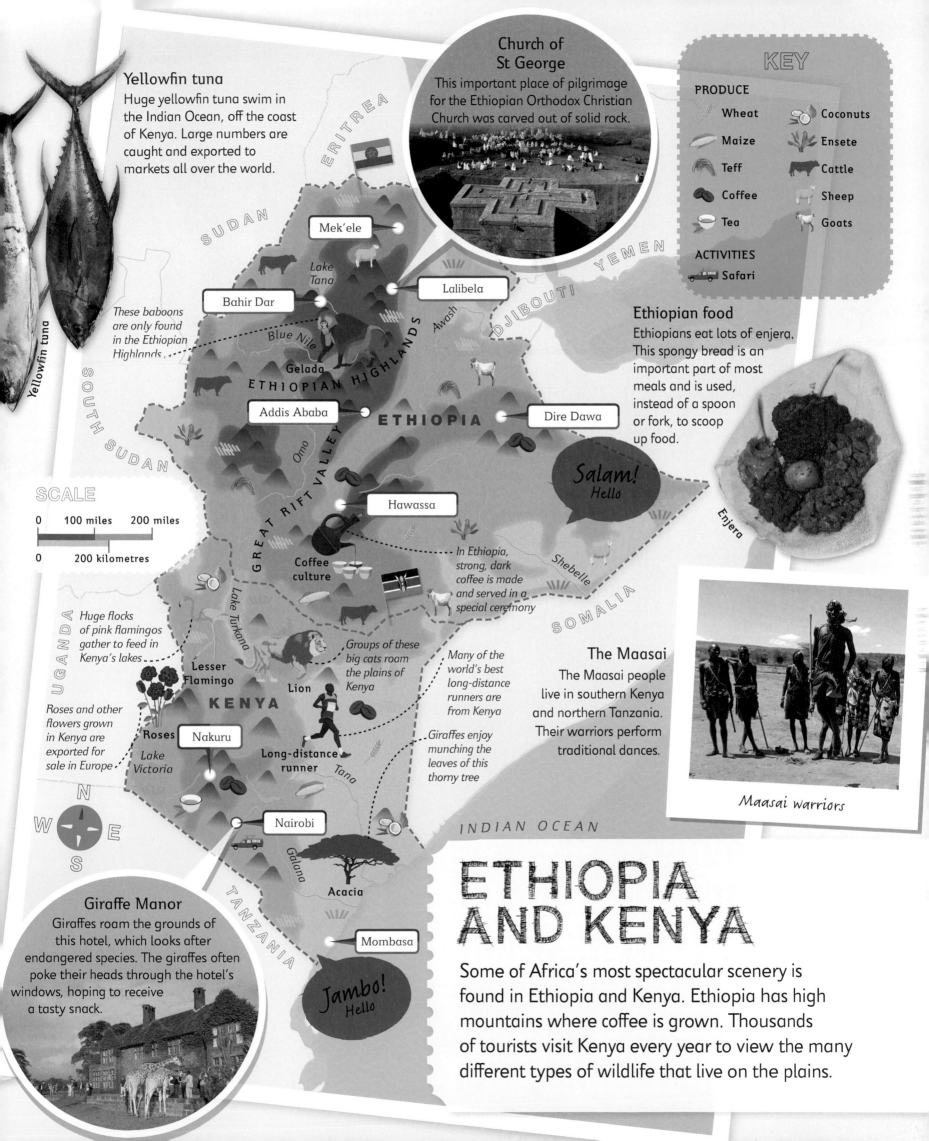

Yellowfin tuna
Huge yellowfin tuna swim in the Indian Ocean, off the coast of Kenya. Large numbers are caught and exported to markets all over the world.

Yellowfin tuna

Church of St George
This important place of pilgrimage for the Ethiopian Orthodox Christian Church was carved out of solid rock.

KEY

PRODUCE

Wheat	Coconuts
Maize	Ensete
Teff	Cattle
Coffee	Sheep
Tea	Goats

ACTIVITIES

Safari

Ethiopian food
Ethiopians eat lots of enjera. This spongy bread is an important part of most meals and is used, instead of a spoon or fork, to scoop up food.

Enjera

ERITREA

SUDAN

SOUTH SUDAN

Mek'ele

Lake Tana

Bahir Dar

These baboons are only found in the Ethiopian Highlands.

Blue Nile

Gelada

ETHIOPIAN HIGHLANDS

Lalibela

Awash

DJIBOUTI

YEMEN

Addis Ababa

ETHIOPIA

Dire Dawa

Omo

GREAT RIFT VALLEY

Hawassa

Coffee culture

In Ethiopia, strong, dark coffee is made and served in a special ceremony

Shebelle

Salam! Hello

SOMALIA

SCALE

0	100 miles	200 miles

0	200 kilometres

UGANDA

Huge flocks of pink flamingos gather to feed in Kenya's lakes

Lake Turkana

Lesser Flamingo

Lion

Groups of these big cats roam the plains of Kenya

Many of the world's best long-distance runners are from Kenya

The Maasai
The Maasai people live in southern Kenya and northern Tanzania. Their warriors perform traditional dances.

Roses and other flowers grown in Kenya are exported for sale in Europe

Roses

KENYA

Nakuru

Lake Victoria

Long-distance runner

Tana

Giraffes enjoy munching the leaves of this thorny tree

Maasai warriors

N W E S

Nairobi

Galana

Acacia

INDIAN OCEAN

Giraffe Manor
Giraffes roam the grounds of this hotel, which looks after endangered species. The giraffes often poke their heads through the hotel's windows, hoping to receive a tasty snack.

TANZANIA

Mombasa

Jambo! Hello

ETHIOPIA AND KENYA

Some of Africa's most spectacular scenery is found in Ethiopia and Kenya. Ethiopia has high mountains where coffee is grown. Thousands of tourists visit Kenya every year to view the many different types of wildlife that live on the plains.

NIGERIA

About 186 million people live in Nigeria, more than in any other African country. Many different tribal groups live here, each with their own colourful traditions, handicrafts, and music. Nigeria is also Africa's largest producer of oil, and has several oil rigs in the Gulf of Guinea.

Tribal traditions
The Yoruba are one of Nigeria's largest tribal groups. Their traditional dress includes brightly patterned fabrics and beautiful, finely carved ivory bracelets.

Ivory bracelet

Yoruba cloth

Hello!

KEY

PRODUCE

Cocoa		Yams	
Rubber		Cotton	
Palm oil		Cattle	
Peanuts		Goats	

INDUSTRY

Oil

Hydroelectric power

NIGER

CHAD

Sokoto

Sokoto

Hadejia

Maiduguri

Kano

This massive rock rises 725 m (2,379 ft) above the countryside to the north of the capital

NIGERIA

Gongola

Lake Kainji

Kaduna

Jos

Zuma rock

Abuja

Falling 150 m (492 ft), Farin Ruwa is one of the highest waterfalls in Nigeria

Sacred Yoruba statues stand among the trees in this area of thick jungle

Niger

Benue

SHEBSHI MOUNTAINS

Wooden mask

BENIN

Ogbomosho

Osun-Osogbo Sacred Grove

Farin Ruwa waterfall

GOTEL MOUNTAINS

Ritual masks
Wooden masks are traditionally worn in parts of Nigeria to ward off evil spirits.

Ibadan

Afrobeat

Afrobeat music combines jazz with chanting and drumming

Lagos

Benin bronzes

Benin City

More than 1,000 bronze plaques once decorated the Royal Palace of the kingdom of Benin

CAMEROON

Pepper sauce

Street food
Nigerian street food includes some spicy dishes. Jollof rice contains chilli, and suya is strips of barbequed meat on a stick with different spices in the seasoning.

GULF OF GUINEA

Aba

Port Harcourt

SCALE

0	100 miles	200 miles
0		200 kilometres

N W E S

Jollof rice

Suya

42

GHANA AND THE IVORY COAST

Ghana was once known as the Gold Coast because of its plentiful gold, and the Ivory Coast used to be a centre for the trade in ivory (elephant tusks). Today, both countries grow cocoa beans, which are used to make some of the world's finest chocolate.

Plantain and okra

West Africa has lots of fertile farming land. Plantains, a type of banana used in cooking, are grown. Another common crop is okra. This is a long, thin vegetable that is often known as "ladies' fingers".

Plantain

KEY

PRODUCE

- Coffee
- Maize
- Cocoa
- Coconuts
- Bananas
- Yams
- Pineapples
- Cassavas
- Rubber
- Cattle
- Palm oil
- Goats
- Rice

INDUSTRY

- Iron
- Oil
- Gold
- Natural gas
- Bauxite
- Diamonds

SCALE

0   50 miles   100 miles

0   100 kilometres

Okra

IVORY COAST

Odienné

Bonjour!
Hello

Katiola

This Roman Catholic basilica is one of the world's largest churches

Daloa

Our Lady of Peace

Yamoussoukro

Bondoukou

GUINEA

LIBERIA

Bandama

Komoé

Lake Kossou

Sassandra

This is a protected area of tropical rainforest and pygmy hippopotamuses make their home here

Taï National Park

Abobo

Football

Ivory Coast's football team is one of the best in Africa

Abidjan

Sekondi-Takoradi

Tuna

Large numbers of tuna are fished in the Gulf of Guinea

These elephants only live in thick rainforests in West and Central Africa

African forest elephants

White Volta

Black Volta

Hello!
Hello

Tamale

GHANA

Kumasi

Kente cloth

Oti

Lake Volta

Volta

TOGO

Kwame Nkrumah Memorial

Accra

Nkrumah led Ghana to independence in 1957.

This colourful cloth is made from cotton and silk

GULF OF GUINEA

Voodoo festivals

Festivals celebrating the traditional voodoo religion take place in southern Ghana. People paint patterns on their faces using white paint.

Typical voodoo facepaint

Pygmy hippopotamus

This small hippopotamus lives in the forests and swamps of West Africa. It only ventures out at night, so is rarely seen.

43

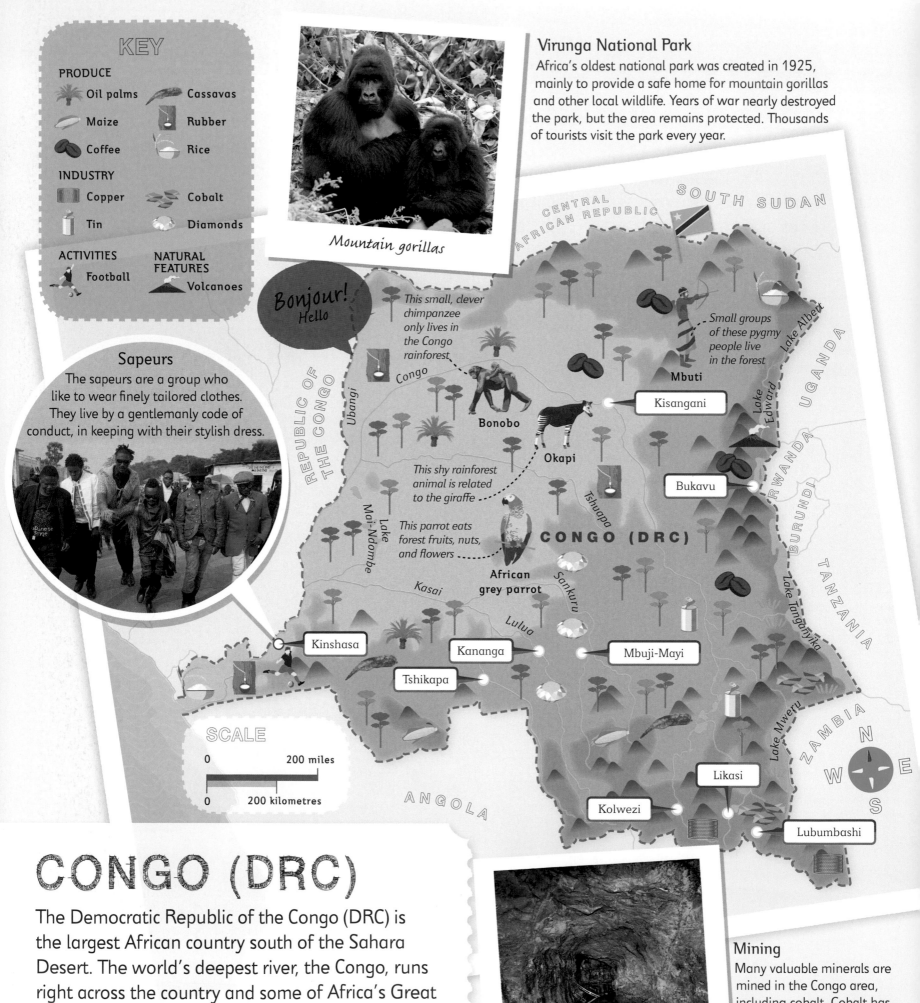

KEY

PRODUCE
- Oil palms
- Cassavas
- Maize
- Rubber
- Coffee
- Rice

INDUSTRY
- Copper
- Cobalt
- Tin
- Diamonds

ACTIVITIES
- Football

NATURAL FEATURES
- Volcanoes

Virunga National Park

Africa's oldest national park was created in 1925, mainly to provide a safe home for mountain gorillas and other local wildlife. Years of war nearly destroyed the park, but the area remains protected. Thousands of tourists visit the park every year.

Mountain gorillas

Sapeurs

The sapeurs are a group who like to wear finely tailored clothes. They live by a gentlemanly code of conduct, in keeping with their stylish dress.

Bonjour! Hello

CENTRAL AFRICAN REPUBLIC

SOUTH SUDAN

REPUBLIC OF THE CONGO

This small, clever chimpanzee only lives in the Congo rainforest

Small groups of these pygmy people live in the forest

Mbuti

Kisangani

Bonobo

Okapi

This shy rainforest animal is related to the giraffe

Bukavu

CONGO (DRC)

This parrot eats forest fruits, nuts, and flowers

African grey parrot

Ubangi

Congo

Lake Mai-Ndombe

Kasai

Lulua

Sankuru

Tshuapa

Lake Albert

Lake Edward

UGANDA

RWANDA

BURUNDI

TANZANIA

Lake Tanganyika

Kinshasa

Kananga

Mbuji-Mayi

Tshikapa

ANGOLA

Lake Mweru

ZAMBIA

Likasi

Kolwezi

Lubumbashi

SCALE

0   200 miles

0   200 kilometres

N E S W

CONGO (DRC)

The Democratic Republic of the Congo (DRC) is the largest African country south of the Sahara Desert. The world's deepest river, the Congo, runs right across the country and some of Africa's Great Lakes lie on its eastern border. The Congo rainforest is the second largest in the world.

Cobalt mine

Mining

Many valuable minerals are mined in the Congo area, including cobalt. Cobalt has been used since ancient times to give a rich blue colour to paints. It is also used in medicine, batteries, and electronic equipment.

ZAMBIA AND ZIMBABWE

Zambia and Zimbabwe are famous for their spectacular scenery and wildlife. Africa's fourth longest river, the Zambezi, flows down through Zambia, then curves along the border with Zimbabwe on its journey to the Indian Ocean.

Southern yellow-billed hornbill

This bird uses its huge beak to snatch up insects, spiders, and even scorpions from the ground. It sleeps in trees at night to avoid predators.

CONGO (DRC)

TANZANIA

MALAWI

Lake Mweru

Lake Tanganyika

Luangwa

Lake Bangweulu

Nshima is a thick maize porridge that is served with vegetables or meat

Nshima

Guides take visitors on walking safaris to get closer to wildlife

Walking safari

SCALE

0 — 200 miles

0 — 200 kilometres

Chingola

Ndola

ZAMBIA

Muli shani!
Hello

Zambezi

Kafue

Kabwe

Lusaka

Leopard

Leopards hunt at night and often carry their prey up into trees to eat

Mhoro!
Hello

This museum has a large collection of old steam engines and carriages

Railway Museum

Livingstone

Victoria Falls

Lake Kariba

Zambezi

ANGOLA

BOTSWANA

MOZAMBIQUE

Harare

Chitungwiza

ZIMBABWE

Gweru

Natural rock formations like this are found in many parts of Zimbabwe

Balancing Rocks

These ruins are the remains of an ancient city

Bulawayo

Cassava

This rhino is in danger of extinction in the wild

Great Zimbabwe

Black rhino

Victoria Falls

The world's largest waterfall is 108 m (354 ft) high and 1,708 m (5,604 ft) wide. The local name is Mosi-oa-Tunya ("the smoke that thunders").

KEY

PRODUCE

- Maize
- Cassavas
- Sweet potatoes
- Millet
- Peanuts
- Roses
- Soya beans
- Cotton

INDUSTRY

- Coal
- Chromium
- Copper
- Platinum
- Nickel
- Hydroelectric power

ACTIVITIES

- Football
- Cricket
- White-water rafting
- Safari

Sweet potato

Root vegetables

Cassavas and sweet potatoes are a main part of people's diet here. Cassava root may be cooked or made into flour that is used to make bread. Sweet potatoes are often boiled or roasted.

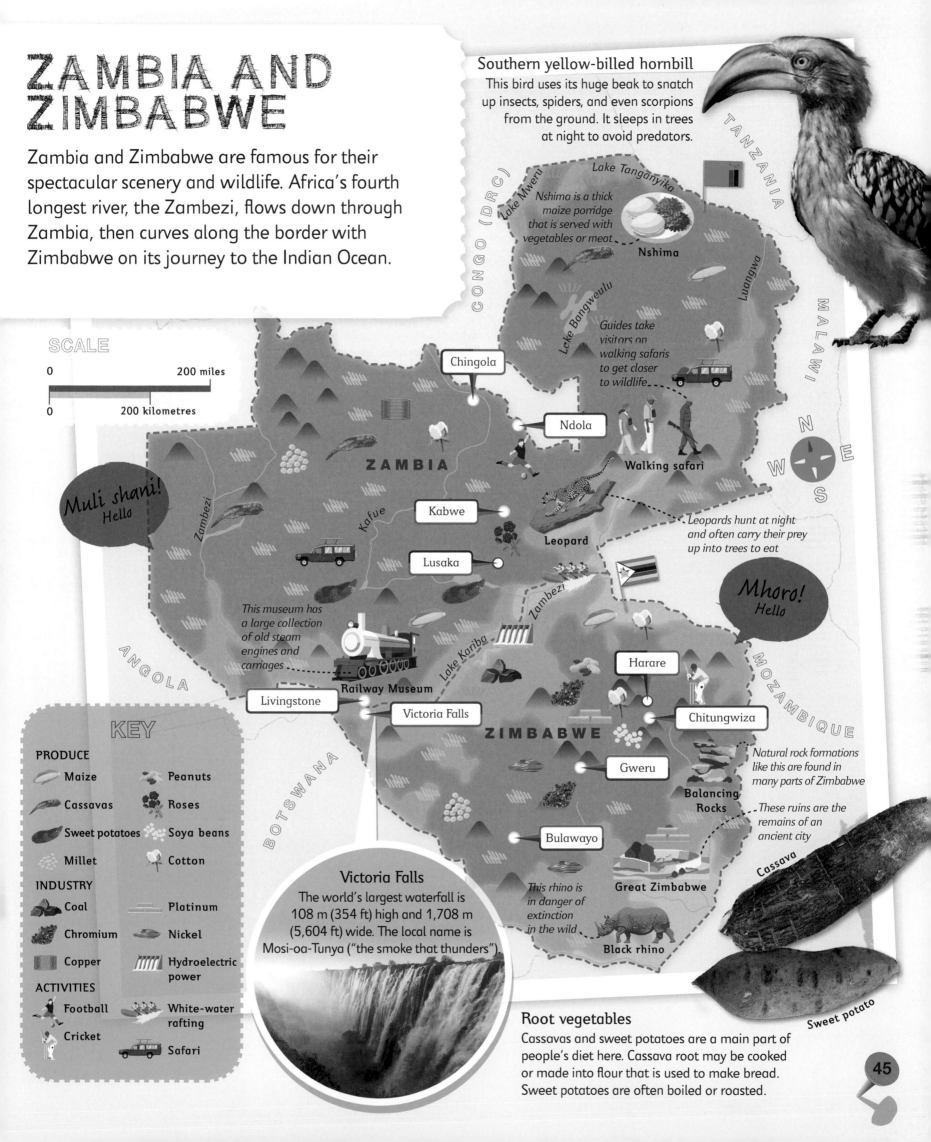

SOUTH AFRICA

South Africa is home to people from many different cultures, which is why it has 11 official languages. The landscape is equally varied, ranging from forests to deserts, and the 2,800-km (1,740-mile) coastline has many lovely beaches.

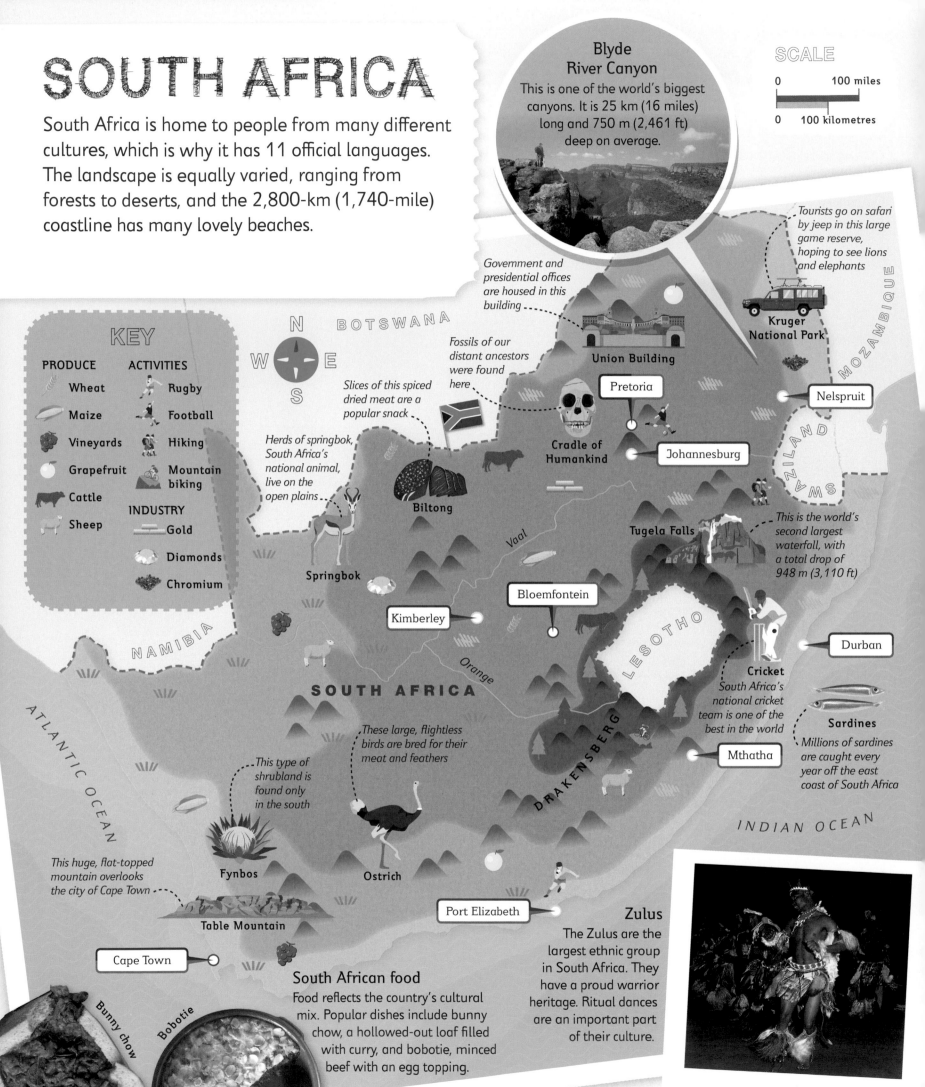

Blyde River Canyon
This is one of the world's biggest canyons. It is 25 km (16 miles) long and 750 m (2,461 ft) deep on average.

SCALE
0   100 miles
0   100 kilometres

BOTSWANA

MOZAMBIQUE

Tourists go on safari by jeep in this large game reserve, hoping to see lions and elephants

Kruger National Park

Government and presidential offices are housed in this building

Union Building

Fossils of our distant ancestors were found here

KEY

PRODUCE
- Wheat
- Maize
- Vineyards
- Grapefruit
- Cattle
- Sheep

ACTIVITIES
- Rugby
- Football
- Hiking
- Mountain biking

INDUSTRY
- Gold
- Diamonds
- Chromium

N W E S

Slices of this spiced dried meat are a popular snack

Herds of springbok, South Africa's national animal, live on the open plains

Biltong

Pretoria

Cradle of Humankind

Johannesburg

Nelspruit

SWAZILAND

This is the world's second largest waterfall, with a total drop of 948 m (3,110 ft)

Tugela Falls

Springbok

Vaal

Bloemfontein

LESOTHO

Kimberley

NAMIBIA

SOUTH AFRICA

Orange

DRAKENSBERG

Durban

Cricket
South Africa's national cricket team is one of the best in the world

Sardines
Millions of sardines are caught every year off the east coast of South Africa

Mthatha

INDIAN OCEAN

These large, flightless birds are bred for their meat and feathers

This type of shrubland is found only in the south

ATLANTIC OCEAN

Fynbos

Ostrich

This huge, flat-topped mountain overlooks the city of Cape Town

Table Mountain

Port Elizabeth

Cape Town

South African food
Food reflects the country's cultural mix. Popular dishes include bunny chow, a hollowed-out loaf filled with curry, and bobotie, minced beef with an egg topping.

Bunny chow

Bobotie

Zulus
The Zulus are the largest ethnic group in South Africa. They have a proud warrior heritage. Ritual dances are an important part of their culture.

Zulu dancer

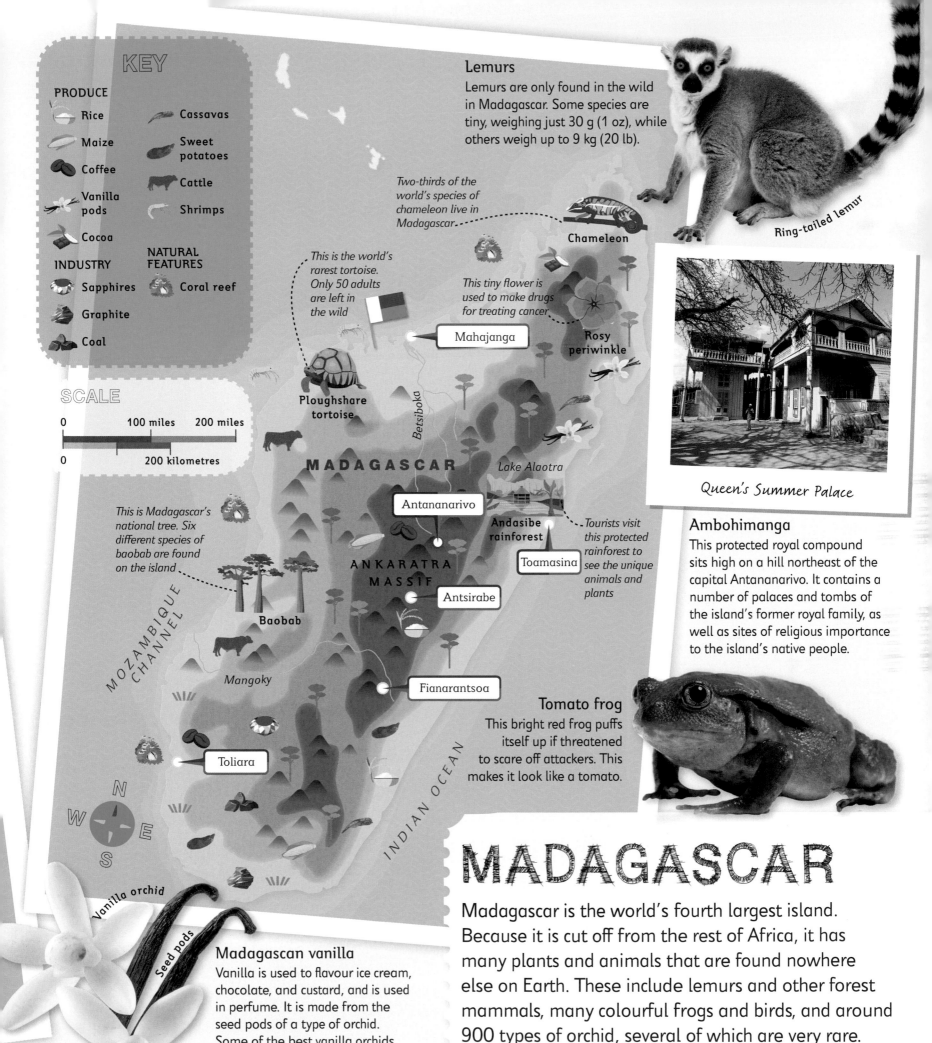

KEY

PRODUCE
- Rice
- Maize
- Coffee
- Vanilla pods
- Cocoa
- Cassavas
- Sweet potatoes
- Cattle
- Shrimps

INDUSTRY
- Sapphires
- Graphite
- Coal

NATURAL FEATURES
- Coral reef

SCALE

0   100 miles   200 miles

0   200 kilometres

Lemurs

Lemurs are only found in the wild in Madagascar. Some species are tiny, weighing just 30 g (1 oz), while others weigh up to 9 kg (20 lb).

Ring-tailed lemur

Two-thirds of the world's species of chameleon live in Madagascar

Chameleon

This is the world's rarest tortoise. Only 50 adults are left in the wild

This tiny flower is used to make drugs for treating cancer

Ploughshare tortoise

Mahajanga

Rosy periwinkle

Betsiboka

MADAGASCAR

Lake Alaotra

This is Madagascar's national tree. Six different species of baobab are found on the island

Antananarivo

Andasibe rainforest

Tourists visit this protected rainforest to see the unique animals and plants

Toamasina

ANKARATRA MASSIF

Antsirabe

Baobab

Fianarantsoa

Mangoky

Toliara

INDIAN OCEAN

N W E S

Vanilla orchid

Seed pods

Queen's Summer Palace

Ambohimanga

This protected royal compound sits high on a hill northeast of the capital Antananarivo. It contains a number of palaces and tombs of the island's former royal family, as well as sites of religious importance to the island's native people.

Tomato frog

This bright red frog puffs itself up if threatened to scare off attackers. This makes it look like a tomato.

Madagascan vanilla

Vanilla is used to flavour ice cream, chocolate, and custard, and is used in perfume. It is made from the seed pods of a type of orchid. Some of the best vanilla orchids are grown in Madagascar.

MADAGASCAR

Madagascar is the world's fourth largest island. Because it is cut off from the rest of Africa, it has many plants and animals that are found nowhere else on Earth. These include lemurs and other forest mammals, many colourful frogs and birds, and around 900 types of orchid, several of which are very rare.

NATURAL WONDERS

The world is full of wonderful natural features that are part of the landscape around us. Across the world, there are lush green rainforests, colourful coral reefs, jagged mountains, smouldering volcanoes, and rushing waterfalls. While under the surface of the Earth there are dark caves, from tiny grottos to huge caverns.

The largest rainforest in the world is the Amazon in South America. It covers almost half of the continent.

Seven Natural Wonders

The Seven Natural Wonders of the World are a group of spectacular natural features. They are favourite sites for adventurous people to visit and explore.

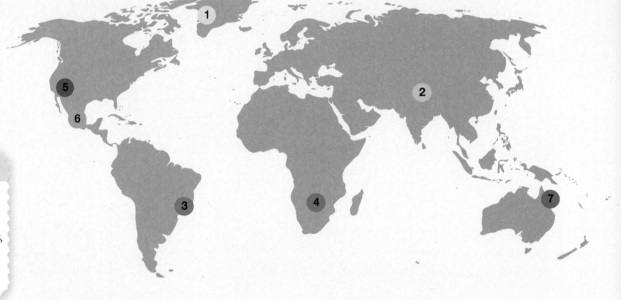

1. NORTHERN LIGHTS

Near the Arctic Circle, amazing light effects known as the Northern Lights, or Aurora Borealis, can be seen in the night sky.

2. MOUNT EVEREST

The world's highest mountain is on the border of Nepal and China. The peak of Mount Everest is a dark pyramid shape.

4. VICTORIA FALLS

Between Zambia and Zimbabwe are the Victoria Falls. The waters of the Zambezi River thunder over these falls.

6. PARÍCUTIN VOLCANO

This volcano rose up and erupted in a farmer's cornfield in Mexico in 1943. Today, people can climb the dormant (inactive) volcano.

3. RIO DE JANEIRO HARBOUR

Here, the Brazilian Highlands meet the Atlantic Ocean. Sugar Loaf Mountain marks the entrance of the bay.

5. GRAND CANYON

In Arizona, USA, the Colorado River has formed the massive and majestic Grand Canyon. This is the largest canyon in the world.

7. GREAT BARRIER REEF

The world's largest coral reef is off the eastern coast of Australia. Thousands of types of fish and coral live here.

Deepest caves

Caves are underground spaces below the surface of Earth. They form when water wears away some types of rock in the ground. This illustration shows some of the deepest caves in the world.

The longest cave is Mammoth Cave, Kentucky, USA. It is 651.8 km (405 miles) long.

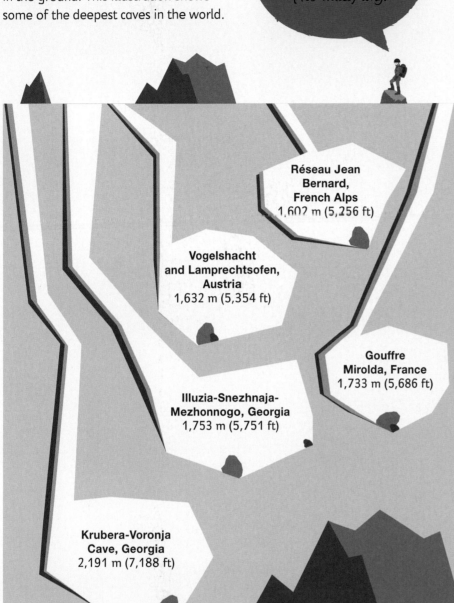

Réseau Jean Bernard, French Alps
1,602 m (5,256 ft)

Vogelshacht and Lamprechtsofen, Austria
1,632 m (5,354 ft)

Gouffre Mirolda, France
1,733 m (5,686 ft)

Illuzia-Snezhnaja-Mezhonnogo, Georgia
1,753 m (5,751 ft)

Krubera-Voronja Cave, Georgia
2,191 m (7,188 ft)

Highest waterfalls

Waterfalls are places where streams of water have a steep drop. They are formed when streams or rivers flow over different types of rock and softer rock is worn away. The five shown below are among the highest waterfalls in the world.

Angel Falls, Venezuela
979 m (3,212 ft)

Tugela Falls, South Africa
948 m (3,110 ft)

Browne Falls, New Zealand
836 m (2,743 ft)

Ramnefjellsfossen, Norway
818 m (2,684 ft)

Cataratas Gocta, Peru
771 m (2,530 ft)

Five largest deserts

Deserts are areas with very little rainfall. They are found in hot, dry regions of the world and also in cold, dry areas, such as around the North and South Poles. This illustration shows the largest deserts in the world.

ANTARCTIC DESERT
14.8 million sq km
(5.7 million sq miles)

SAHARA DESERT
9 million sq km
(3.5 million sq miles)

ARABIAN DESERT
2.3 million sq km
(0.9 million sq miles)

KALAHARI DESERT
0.9 million sq km
(0.36 million sq miles)

GOBI DESERT
1.3 million sq km
(0.5 million sq miles)

49

1. On which island was Napoleon born?

2. What is the name of this colourful building in Moscow?

3. In which country would you find this angelic statue?

4. Which city was the composer Mozart born in?

EUROPE

With many unique cultures and languages, Europe is a varied continent. It is the home of classical music, great literature, and fine art and architecture. It has medieval castles and cathedrals, as well as beautiful historic towns and cities.

8. Where would you find flamenco dancers?

7. Which river does this bridge go across?

5. Which country is the car maker Skoda based in?

6. Which country produces more than 400 kinds of cheese?

You can find all the answers and more quizzes on pages 120-121.

EUROPE

The landscape of Europe is full of contrasts. It includes high mountain ranges, dense forests, sandy beaches, and large sweeps of flat, fertile farmland. Countries range in size from the tiny state of Liechtenstein to Russia, the biggest country in the world.

Northern European forest

The pine forests of Nordic countries such as Norway, Sweden, and Finland are an important source of timber.

Paris

Paris, the capital of France, is an elegant city that mixes old and new styles of architecture effortlessly. At its centre is the Eiffel Tower, one of the most famous structures on Earth.

Mediterranean Sea

The countries that surround the warm waters of the Mediterranean Sea enjoy hot, dry summers and mild winters. Thousands of visitors are drawn to their sunny beaches every year.

ICELAND

ATLANTIC OCEAN

NORWEGIAN SEA

Faroe Islands

Shetland Islands

NORWAY

SWEDEN

NORTH SEA

DENMARK

Bornho

IRELAND

Isle of Man

UNITED KINGDOM

NETHERLANDS

BELGIUM

GERMANY

LUXEMBOURG

CZECH REPUBLIC

Channel Islands

LIECHTENSTEIN

BAY OF BISCAY

FRANCE

SWITZERLAND

AUSTRI

SLOVENI

Azores

SAN MARINO

ADRIATIC SE

CROAT

PORTUGAL

ANDORRA

MONACO

ITALY

SPAIN

Corsica

VATICAN CITY

Majorca
Ibiza   Minorca

Sardinia

Gibraltar

Balearic Islands

TYRRHENIAN SEA

Madeira

MEDITERRANEAN SEA

Sicily

MALT

SCALE

0   250 miles   500 miles

0   500 kilometres

GULF OF BOTHNIA

FINLAND

Gotland

BALTIC SEA

ESTONIA

LATVIA

LITHUANIA

RUSSIA
(KALININGRAD)

BELARUS

POLAND

RUSSIA
(European Russia)

UKRAINE

LOVAKIA

HUNGARY

MOLDOVA

ROMANIA

Crimea

HERZEGOVINA

MONTENEGRO

SERBIA

KOSOVO
(DISPUTED)

BULGARIA

BLACK SEA

ALBANIA

MACEDONIA

TURKEY

AEGEAN
SEA

GREECE

IONIAN
SEA

Crete

CASPIAN SEA

The Alps
This mountain range stretches 1,200 km
(750 miles) across the heart of Europe,
through France, Monaco, Italy, Germany,
Austria, Switzerland, Liechtenstein, and
Slovenia. The highest peak is Mont Blanc
at 4,810 m (15,781 ft).

St Basil's Cathedral
This spectacular building dominates
Red Square in Moscow. It was built
in the 16th century and is famous
for its unique, brightly coloured,
onion-shaped domes. It has
been a museum since 1928.

NORTHERN EUROPE

The northern European countries have fairly small populations, with most people living in towns and cities. There are also large areas of unspoilt countryside. Summers are generally warm, but winters are very cold, with limited daylight in the far north.

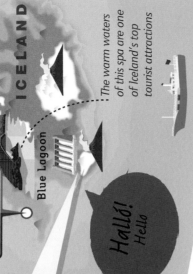

This fox grows a white coat in winter to blend into the snow.

Arctic fox

ICELAND

Reykjavik

Blue Lagoon

The warm waters of this spa are one of Iceland's top tourist attractions

Halló!
Hello

Eyjafjallajökull

This huge volcano in Iceland is covered by an ice cap. It erupted in 2010, producing a vast ash cloud that disrupted air travel across Europe.

Sami in traditional dress

Lapland

This large, snowy region in the far north of Norway, Sweden, and Finland is home to the Sami people. Some keep reindeer and ride around in sleighs.

SCALE

0 — 100 miles

0 — 100 kilometres

Elk

The elk is the largest type of deer in the world and lives in northern forests

Oulu

Alstom Pendolino

This fast train tilts when it goes around corners

Wolverine

This strong, ferocious animal can kill prey as big as deer

Tromsø

N W E S

EV plug-in electric car

These cars are very popular in Norway. They are plugged in to be recharged

Abisko National Park

Kiruna

This park contains Trollsjön lake, the clearest lake in Sweden

Lynx

This wild cat lives in forests, where it hunts deer and other animals

NORWEGIAN SEA

Pulpit Rock overlooking Lysefjord

Norway's fjords

Norway's coast is lined with hundreds of narrow inlets, called fjords, with steep cliffs on each side. The cliffs of Pulpit Rock rise a spectacular 604 m (1,982 ft) above the waters of Lysefjord.

Rollmop

These snacks are made from pickled herring fish fillets rolled into a cylinder shape around a tasty filling, such as olives and pickled gherkins.

KEY

PRODUCE

Sheep
Cattle
Potatoes
Rye
Wheat
Sugar beet
Barley
Pigs

ACTIVITIES

Ice hockey
Football
Cross-country skiing

INDUSTRY

Timber
Shipbuilding
Hydroelectric power
Natural gas
Oil
Fishing
Wind power
Iron ore
Electronics

NATURAL FEATURES

Volcanoes

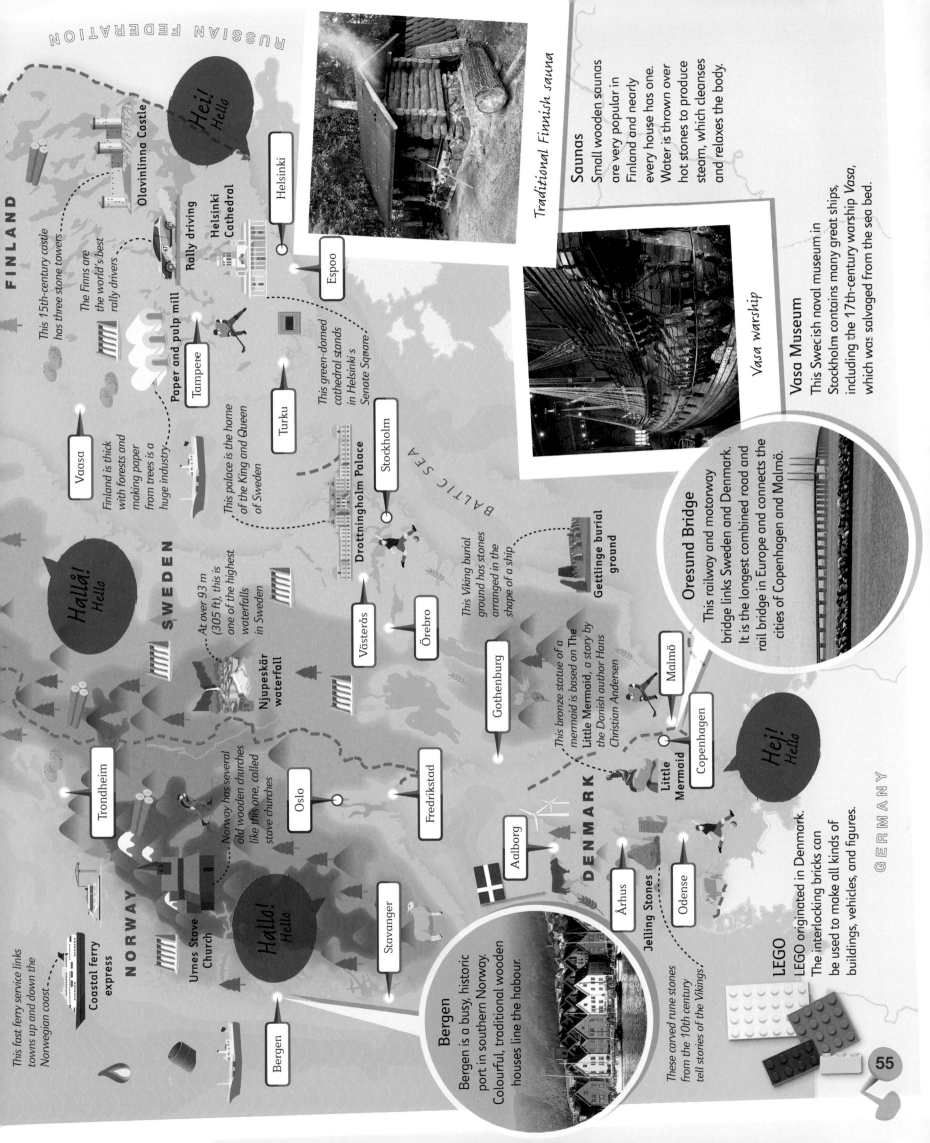

FINLAND

Hei!
Hello

Olavinlinna Castle

This 15th-century castle has three stone towers

The Finns are the world's best rally drivers

Rally driving

Helsinki Cathedral

Helsinki

Espoo

Paper and pulp mill

Tampere

Finland is thick with forests and making paper from trees is a huge industry

Vaasa

Turku

This green-domed cathedral stands in Helsinki's Senate Square

Traditional Finnish sauna

Saunas

Small wooden saunas are very popular in Finland and nearly every house has one. Water is thrown over hot stones to produce steam, which cleanses and relaxes the body.

Vasa warship

Vasa Museum

This Swedish naval museum in Stockholm contains many great ships, including the 17th-century warship *Vasa*, which was salvaged from the sea bed.

SWEDEN

Hallå!
Hello

At over 93 m (305 ft), this is one of the highest waterfalls in Sweden

This palace is the home of the King and Queen of Sweden

Drottningholm Palace

Stockholm

BALTIC SEA

Njupeskär waterfall

Västerås

Örebro

This Viking burial ground has stones arranged in the shape of a ship

Gettlinge burial ground

Gothenburg

This bronze statue of a mermaid is based on The Little Mermaid, a story by the Danish author Hans Christian Andersen

Øresund Bridge

This railway and motorway bridge links Sweden and Denmark. It is the longest combined road and rail bridge in Europe and connects the cities of Copenhagen and Malmö.

Malmö

Little Mermaid

Copenhagen

Hej!
Hello

NORWAY

Hallo!
Hello

This fast ferry service links towns up and down the Norwegian coast

Coastal ferry express

Trondheim

Norway has several old wooden churches like this one, called stave churches

Urnes Stave Church

Oslo

Fredrikstad

Stavanger

Bergen

Bergen

Bergen is a busy, historic port in southern Norway. Colourful, traditional wooden houses line the habour.

DENMARK

Aalborg

Århus

Odense

Jelling Stones

These carved rune stones from the 10th century tell stories of the Vikings.

LEGO

LEGO originated in Denmark. The interlocking bricks can be used to make all kinds of buildings, vehicles, and figures.

GERMANY

55

BRITISH ISLES

The British Isles is a small group of islands off the northwest coast of Europe. They consist of the United Kingdom, or UK (England, Scotland, Wales, and Northern Ireland), and Ireland. These islands are rich in history and tradition. The weather is influenced by the sea and it often rains. In fact, Ireland is known as the "Emerald Isle", because the rain makes it so green.

Fish and chips

Tea

Food and drink

Fried fish and chips are a popular meal, especially by the coast. Tea is widely drunk, usually with milk and sometimes sugar.

William Shakespeare

English playwright

William Shakespeare was one of the world's greatest writers. Born in Stratford-upon-Avon, England, in 1564, he wrote many poems and plays that are still performed today.

Scottish traditions

For special occasions, some Scots wear woollen kilts, woven from different coloured threads to form a pattern known as tartan. Different clans (groups) have their own design of tartan. Some Scots also play the bagpipes, a type of wind instrument.

Traditional Scottish dress

Shetland Islands

Orkney Islands

Most of the UK's red squirrels live in the pine forests of Scotland

Aberdeen

Red squirrel

This popular sport was developed in Scotland

Golf

GRAMPIAN MOUNTAINS

Inverness

Edinburgh Castle

This ancient fortress is built on a prominent rock above the city of Edinburgh

Scotland

Edinburgh

Clyde

Glasgow

Angel of the North

The wings of this huge steel statue are 54 m (177 ft) across

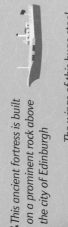
Newcastle-upon-Tyne

Inner Hebrides

Outer Hebrides

ATLANTIC OCEAN

N
W   E
S

This unique rock formation is made up of hexagonal (six-sided) columns formed after an ancient volcanic eruption

Giant's Causeway

Northern Ireland

Belfast

KEY

PRODUCE
- Wheat
- Fruit
- Potatoes
- Sheep
- Shellfish
- Cattle
- Vineyards
- Cheese

INDUSTRY
- Cars
- Fishing

RESOURCES
- Oil
- Gas
- Steel

ACTIVITIES
- Football
- Rock climbing
- Hiking
- Surfing
- Cricket

SCALE

0   50 miles   100 miles

0   100 kilometres

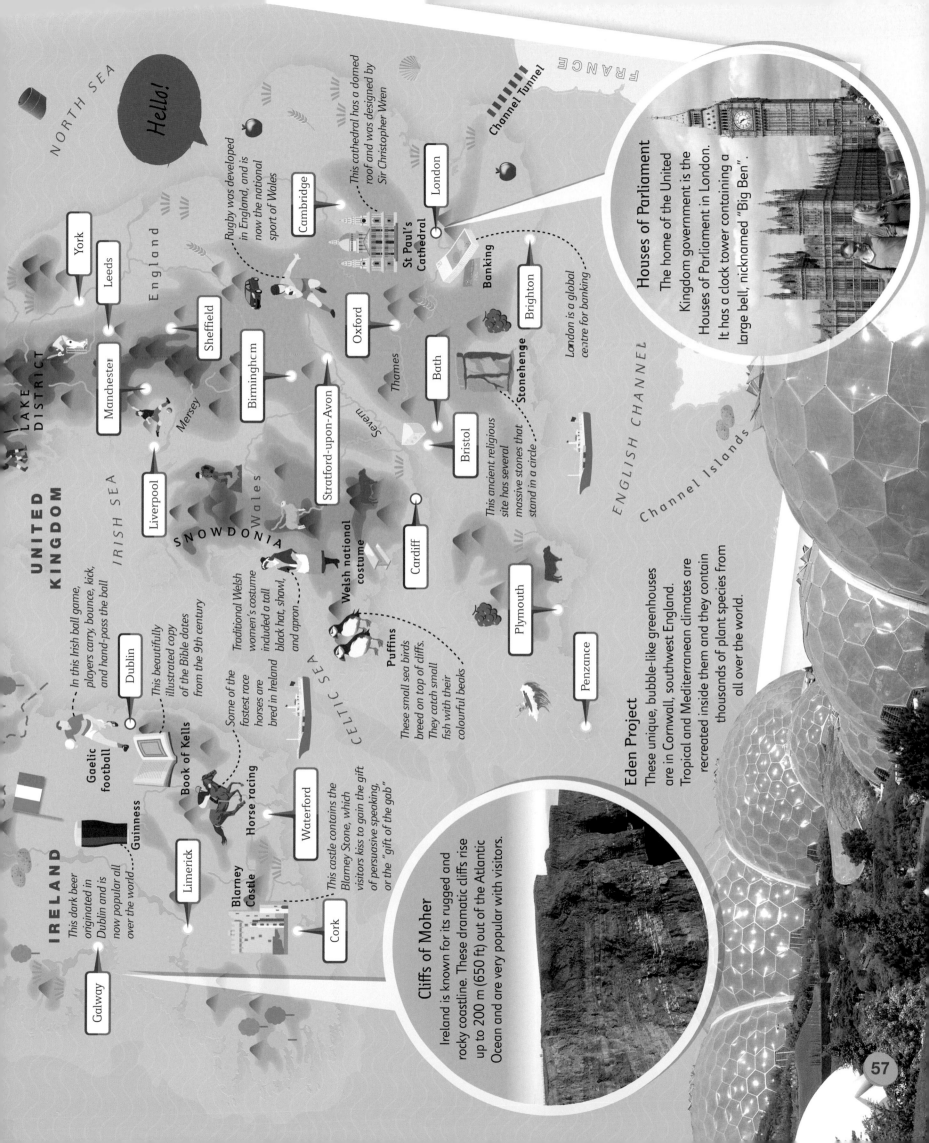

NORTH SEA

Hello!

UNITED KINGDOM

LAKE DISTRICT

IRISH SEA

England

York

Leeds

Manchester

Sheffield

Birmingham

Liverpool

Mersey

SNOWDONIA

Wales

Stratford-upon-Avon

Welsh national costume

Traditional Welsh women's costume included a tall black hat, shawl, and apron.

Cardiff

Cambridge

Rugby was developed in England, and is now the national sport of Wales

This cathedral has a domed roof and was designed by Sir Christopher Wren

St Paul's Cathedral

Oxford

Thames

Severn

Bath

Bristol

Stonehenge

This ancient religious site has several massive stones that stand in a circle

Banking

London is a global centre for banking

Brighton

Channel Tunnel

FRANCE

London

ENGLISH CHANNEL

Channel Islands

Plymouth

Penzance

Puffins

These small sea birds breed on top of cliffs. They catch small fish with their colourful beaks

CELTIC SEA

IRELAND

This dark beer originated in Dublin and is now popular all over the world

Guinness

Galway

Limerick

Blarney Castle

This castle contains the Blarney Stone, which visitors kiss to gain the gift of persuasive speaking, or the "gift of the gab"

Cork

Waterford

Horse racing

Some of the fastest race horses are bred in Ireland

Book of Kells

This beautifully illustrated copy of the Bible dates from the 9th century

Gaelic football

In this Irish ball game, players carry, bounce, kick, and hand-pass the ball

Dublin

Houses of Parliament

The home of the United Kingdom government is the Houses of Parliament in London. It has a clock tower containing a large bell, nicknamed "Big Ben".

Cliffs of Moher

Ireland is known for its rugged and rocky coastline. These dramatic cliffs rise up to 200 m (650 ft) out of the Atlantic Ocean and are very popular with visitors.

Eden Project

These unique, bubble-like greenhouses are in Cornwall, southwest England. Tropical and Mediterranean climates are recreated inside them and they contain thousands of plant species from all over the world.

57

FRANCE

France is known throughout the world for its food and wine and beautiful countryside. Today, most French people live in towns and cities. France is highly industrialized and has one of the fastest train networks, the TGV. The arts, such as painting, and sport, particularly cycling, are very popular.

UNITED KINGDOM

Channel Tunnel

Calais

ENGLISH CHANNEL

This medieval tapestry shows the story of the Norman conquest of England in 1066

Bayeux Tapestry

Rouen

Le Havre

Eiffel Tower

Seine

Completed in 1889, this iron tower is 324 m (1,063 ft) tall including the TV antenna that was added to the top

People can walk to the abbey and houses on this island during low tides

Mont-Saint-Michel

About 3,000 big stones were placed in rows at this ancient site more than 5,000 years ago

Le Mans

This is the largest and grandest château in the Loire

Orléans

Rennes

Carnac stones

Nantes

Loire

Château de Chambord

Art

Millions of people visit France's museums every year to see paintings and sculptures by artists such as Claude Monet and Auguste Rodin.

Water Lilies, by Monet

Loire châteaux

The Loire Valley is famous for its 42 châteaux, or large country houses. Château de Chenonceau sits across the River Cher on a row of arches.

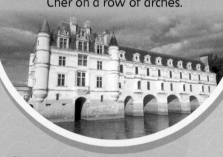

ATLANTIC OCEAN

Humans painted horses and wild cattle on cave walls more than 17,000 years ago

Lascaux caves

Dordogne

Bonjour! Hello

Garonne

Périgord truffles

Bordeaux

These edible fungi sell for hundreds of pounds a kilo

Cheese and wine

More than 400 different cheeses are made in France. Almost every area has its own type, ranging from soft cheeses, such as Camembert, to hard and even blue cheeses. France also produces some of the world's best wines, made from the juice of black or white grapes. Sunflowers are also grown in the south. Their seeds are pressed to make oil.

Bears from Slovenia were moved to the Pyrenees after the last local bear died in 2006

Brown bear

Toulouse

Sunflower

58

Camembert cheese

Grapes

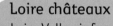

SCALE

0   50 miles   100 miles

0   100 kilometres

PYRENEES

SPAIN

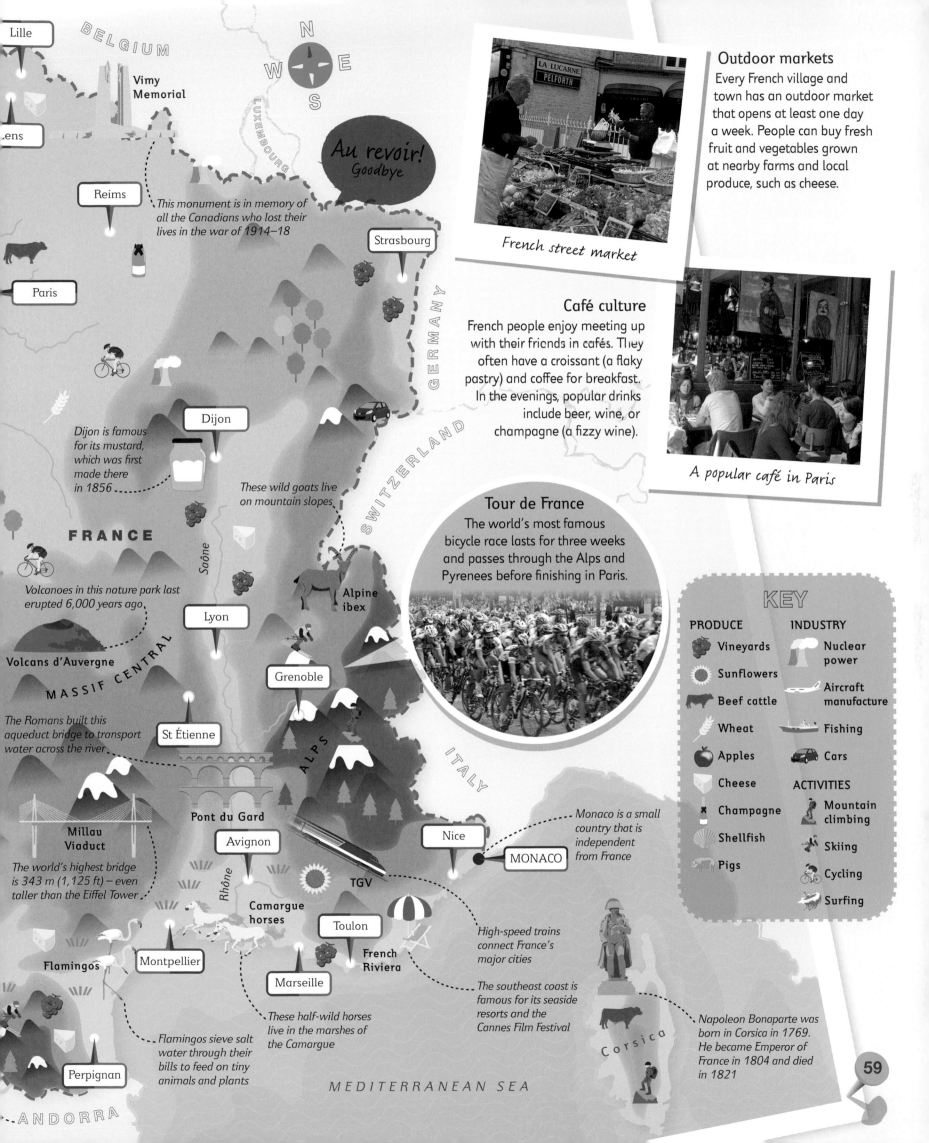

Lille

BELGIUM

Vimy
Memorial

ens

LUXEMBOURG

N
W ⟶ E
S

Au revoir!
Goodbye

Reims

*This monument is in memory of
all the Canadians who lost their
lives in the war of 1914–18*

Strasbourg

Paris

GERMANY

Outdoor markets
Every French village and
town has an outdoor market
that opens at least one day
a week. People can buy fresh
fruit and vegetables grown
at nearby farms and local
produce, such as cheese.

French street market

Dijon

*Dijon is famous
for its mustard,
which was first
made there
in 1856*

SWITZERLAND

*These wild goats live
on mountain slopes*

Café culture
French people enjoy meeting up
with their friends in cafés. They
often have a croissant (a flaky
pastry) and coffee for breakfast.
In the evenings, popular drinks
include beer, wine, or
champagne (a fizzy wine).

A popular café in Paris

FRANCE

Saône

*Volcanoes in this nature park last
erupted 6,000 years ago*

Lyon

Alpine
ibex

Tour de France
The world's most famous
bicycle race lasts for three weeks
and passes through the Alps and
Pyrenees before finishing in Paris.

Volcans d'Auvergne

MASSIF CENTRAL

*The Romans built this
aqueduct bridge to transport
water across the river*

St Étienne

Grenoble

ITALY

ALPS

Millau
Viaduct

Pont du Gard

*The world's highest bridge
is 343 m (1,125 ft) – even
taller than the Eiffel Tower*

Avignon

TGV

Nice

MONACO

*Monaco is a small
country that is
independent
from France*

Rhône

Camargue
horses

Toulon

French
Riviera

*High-speed trains
connect France's
major cities*

KEY

PRODUCE

Vineyards

Sunflowers

Beef cattle

Wheat

Apples

Cheese

Champagne

Shellfish

Pigs

INDUSTRY

Nuclear
power

Aircraft
manufacture

Fishing

Cars

ACTIVITIES

Mountain
climbing

Skiing

Cycling

Surfing

Montpellier

Flamingos

Marseille

*These half-wild horses
live in the marshes of
the Camargue*

*The southeast coast is
famous for its seaside
resorts and the
Cannes Film Festival*

*Napoleon Bonaparte was
born in Corsica in 1769.
He became Emperor of
France in 1804 and died
in 1821*

Corsica

Perpignan

*Flamingos sieve salt
water through their
bills to feed on tiny
animals and plants*

MEDITERRANEAN SEA

ANDORRA

59

NETHERLANDS, BELGIUM, AND LUXEMBOURG

These three countries are known as the Low Countries, because most of the land is flat, with a lot of it at or below sea level. This flat land means cycling is popular. The countries are among the wealthiest in Europe.

NORTH SEA

Wadden Islands

The Netherlands is famous for its tulip farms, most of which are in the northeast of the country

Groningen

Windmills pump water out of wet areas and help protect land from flooding

Windmill

NETHERLANDS

Tulips

This brave girl went into hiding during World War II and kept a diary of her experiences

Anne Frank

Amsterdam
There are many canals in Amsterdam and lots of people live in waterfront apartments. Amsterdam also has several important art galleries.

This building in The Hague is the home of the Dutch government

Amsterdam

The Hague

Binnenhof

Utrecht

Arnhem

Hockey is a major sport in the Netherlands

Field hockey

Rotterdam

This medieval bell tower is in the historic city of Bruges

Antwerp is a centre of the diamond trade

This great artist was born in Zundert in the southern Netherlands in 1853

Vincent van Gogh

Eindhoven

Safe cycling

Ostend

Red poppy flowers grow in the fields of Belgium

Belfry of Bruges

Diamond trade

Antwerp

Bruges

Ghent

Field poppy

HERGÉ
TINTIN ET LES PICAROS
CASTERMAN

Brussels

Belgian lace is known for its beauty and delicacy

Belgian lace

Atomium

This unique building is the symbol of Brussels

Belgian beer

Thousands of different types of beer are brewed across Belgium

Cycling
Cycle lanes are found throughout the Netherlands and Belgium, making it safe and quick for cyclists on the move.

Meuse

Charleroi

Liège

KEY

PRODUCE	INDUSTRY
Potatoes	Steel
Cheese	Gas
Cattle	**ACTIVITIES**
Pigs	Football
Greenhouses	Hiking
Wheat	Cycling
Fruit	Banking

Tintin
The Adventures of Tintin and his dog, Snowy, are told in the comic books written by the Belgian cartoonist Hergé.

Tintin travelled the world and solved many mysteries

Belgian food
Mussels and fries (called *moules* and *frites* in Belgium) is a favourite Belgian dish. Another speciality is rich and creamy Belgian chocolates.

B E L G I U M

F R A N C E

A R D E N N E S

Luxembourg
There are many ancient castles to be found in Luxembourg. This small country is also a major financial centre.

Luxembourg City

L U X E M B O U R G

Vianden Castle in Luxembourg is a popular tourist destination

Moules and frites

SWITZERLAND AND AUSTRIA

Switzerland and Austria are mountainous countries in Central Europe. The Alps run through both countries, providing snow-covered slopes that are used for winter sports and beautiful alpine valleys, where hiking is popular in the summer.

Lipizzaner and rider

Spanish Riding School
The Spanish Riding School in Vienna teaches traditional horse-riding techniques and is home to the Lipizzaner, a breed of white horse.

This cathedral has a multi-coloured roof

CZECH REPUBLIC

SLOVAKIA

Vienna

Linz

Stephansdom

Danube

Neusiedler See

HUNGARY

The great composer Wolfgang Amadeus Mozart was born in Salzburg in 1756

Salzburg

Mozart

Graz

AUSTRIA

SLOVENIA

Le Corbusier
This Swiss-French architect designed stylish modern buildings, often featuring straight lines and bright blocks of colours.

Sachertorte
This rich chocolate cake is served in coffee houses, where Austrians love to meet up. Coffee houses are an important part of Austrian social life, especially in Vienna.

GERMANY

FRANCE

Liechtenstein is one of the smallest countries in the world and specializes in banking

Innsbruck

ALPS

ALPS

Chamois

These wild goats are hunted for their meat

This Swiss author wrote Heidi, a novel about a young girl who lives in the Alps

Zürich

Basel

Johanna Spyri

LIECHTENSTEIN

Gentiana

Bern

The finest watches and clocks are made in Switzerland

Watches

This flower grows in the mountains and is used to flavour drinks

SCALE

0   50 miles

0   50 kilometres

SWITZERLAND

ALPS

ALPS

Lausanne

Alpine horns are used in the mountains to play music or send signals

Geneva

Red Cross

Hornblower

ITALY

Geneva is home to the Red Cross, which provides care to people in need around the world

KEY

PRODUCE
- Cheese
- Cattle
- Vineyards
- Apricots

INDUSTRY
- Timber
- Banking
- Hydroelectric power

ACTIVITIES
- Skiing
- Hiking
- Mountain climbing

Alpine marmot
Marmots live high up in the Alps, eating grass and shrubs. They are sociable little animals, who whistle to each other. In winter, they hibernate in burrows.

Matterhorn
On the Swiss-Italian border is the dramatic Matterhorn. It has a pyramid-shaped peak and is one of the highest mountains in Europe.

Skiing in the Alps
The snowy Alps are great for winter sports, such as skiing and snowboarding. Competitions, such as downhill racing, are held for both children and adults.

Downhill racer

SPAIN AND PORTUGAL

Spain and Portugal are part of sunny southern Europe. Both countries have long coastlines and spectacular scenery, making them popular with holidaymakers. The sea is a major source of food, and fishing is an important industry in both countries.

Many people walk to this cathedral on a pilgrimage

Santiago de Compostela Cathedral

Santiago de Compostela

León

These grey wolves live in the forests and grassy planes of northern Portugal and Spain

Iberian wolf

Esla

This house is decorated with more than 300 scallop shells

Braga

Port is a special type of strong, sweet wine that is made in the Douro Valley

Portuguese tiles

Decorative tiles are found on homes and churches and are sometimes used as street signs. They often show scenes including cities, flowers, and fishing boats.

Decorative tiles

Guimarães

Porto

Port

House of Shells

Douro

Salamanca

These traditional boats from Aveiro have a half-moon shape and are painted in bright colours

Moliceiro boat

Aveiro

Luis de Camoes

This great Portuguese poet lived in the 16th century

Tagus

Fado is traditional Portuguese music that is often accompanied by guitar

Coimbra

Fado

Nazaré

PORTUGAL

Bark is cut from cork trees and used to make wine corks

Cork

Guadiana

Many people visit the Azores to see dolphins

Dolphin watching

Azores

Ponta Delgada

This 16th-century fort sits at the entrance to Lisbon's harbour

Belém Tower

Lisbon

This temple in Evora was once an important place of worship

Roman temple

Badajoz

Madeira

Madeira is a strong type of wine made on the island of Madeira

Madeira and the Azores
These islands in the middle of the Atlantic Ocean belong to Portugal. They are a popular destination for cruise ships to visit.

Setúbal

Evora

Olá!
Hello

Guadiana

Funchal

Canary Islands
These Spanish islands are found off North Africa's west coast.

Santa Cruz de Tenerife

Canary Islands

Seville

Faro

Sherry is a strong type of wine made from white grapes grown in Jerez

Sherry

SCALE

0   100 miles

0   100 kilometres

Las Palmas de Gran Canaria

Jerez de la Frontera

Cádiz

ATLANTIC OCEAN

Guggenheim Museum

San Sebastian

Bilbao

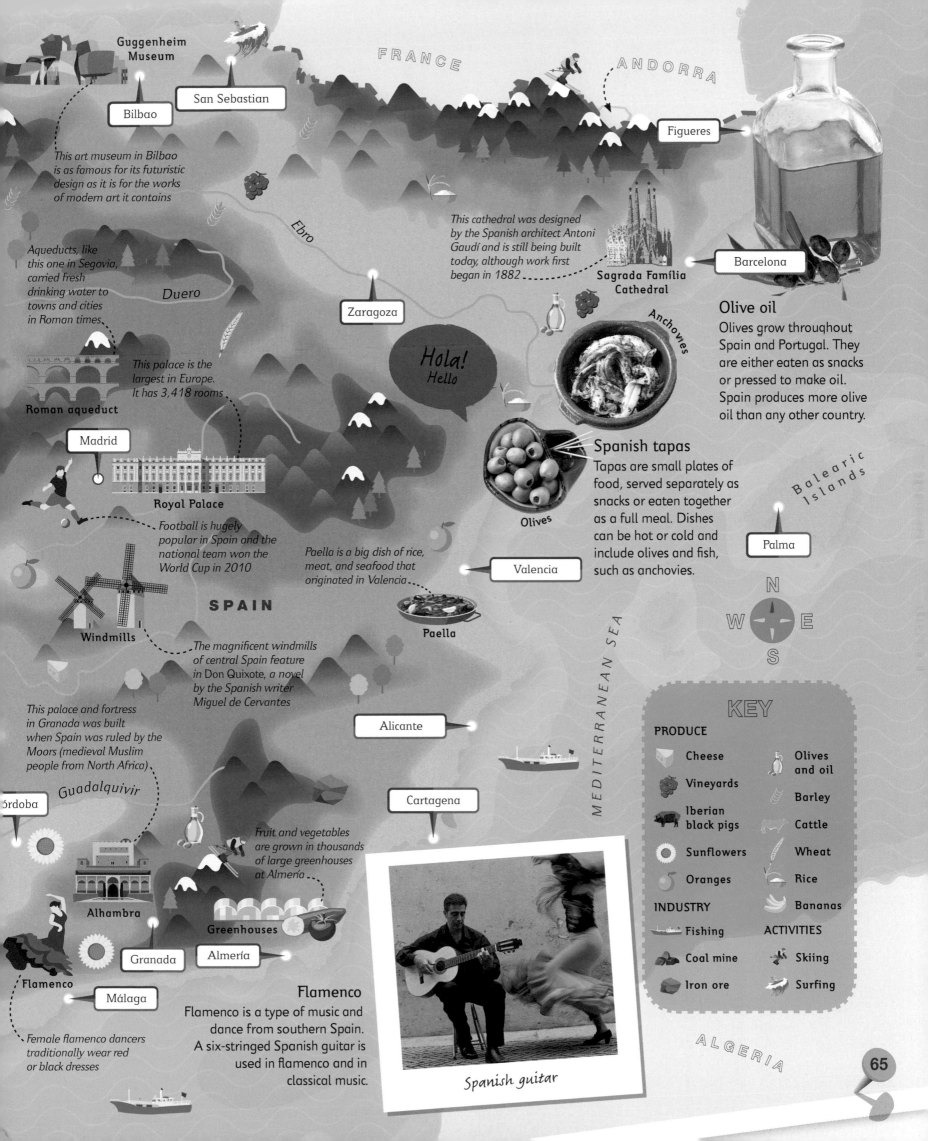

This art museum in Bilbao is as famous for its futuristic design as it is for the works of modern art it contains

FRANCE

ANDORRA

Figueres

Ebro

This cathedral was designed by the Spanish architect Antoni Gaudí and is still being built today, although work first began in 1882

Sagrada Família Cathedral

Barcelona

Aqueducts, like this one in Segovia, carried fresh drinking water to towns and cities in Roman times

Duero

Zaragoza

Anchovies

Olive oil
Olives grow throughout Spain and Portugal. They are either eaten as snacks or pressed to make oil. Spain produces more olive oil than any other country.

Roman aqueduct

This palace is the largest in Europe. It has 3,418 rooms

Hola!
Hello

Madrid

Royal Palace

Football is hugely popular in Spain and the national team won the World Cup in 2010

Olives

Spanish tapas
Tapas are small plates of food, served separately as snacks or eaten together as a full meal. Dishes can be hot or cold and include olives and fish, such as anchovies.

Balearic Islands

Palma

Paella is a big dish of rice, meat, and seafood that originated in Valencia

Valencia

SPAIN

Windmills

The magnificent windmills of central Spain feature in Don Quixote, a novel by the Spanish writer Miguel de Cervantes

Paella

N
W   E
S

This palace and fortress in Granada was built when Spain was ruled by the Moors (medieval Muslim people from North Africa)

Alicante

MEDITERRANEAN SEA

Guadalquivir

Córdoba

Fruit and vegetables are grown in thousands of large greenhouses at Almería

Cartagena

Alhambra

Greenhouses

Granada

Almería

Flamenco

Málaga

Female flamenco dancers traditionally wear red or black dresses

Flamenco
Flamenco is a type of music and dance from southern Spain. A six-stringed Spanish guitar is used in flamenco and in classical music.

Spanish guitar

ALGERIA

KEY

PRODUCE

Cheese

Vineyards

Iberian black pigs

Sunflowers

Oranges

Olives and oil

Barley

Cattle

Wheat

Rice

INDUSTRY

Fishing

Coal mine

Iron ore

Bananas

ACTIVITIES

Skiing

Surfing

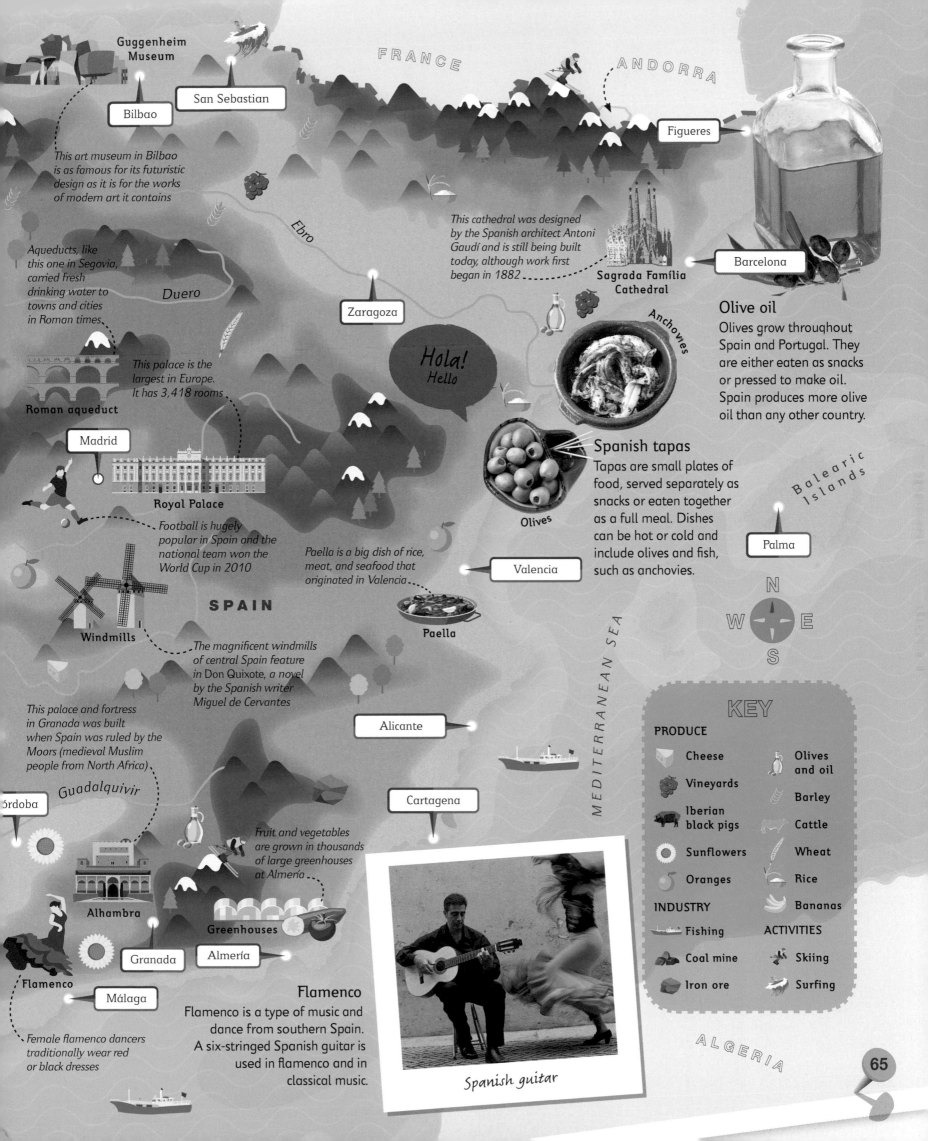

ITALY

Italy stretches down from the Alps in the north to the Mediterranean island of Sicily in the south. The country is shaped like a boot, with its toe almost touching Sicily. In ancient times, the Romans built a great empire that was ruled from Rome. Italy is also famous for its art and architecture.

Scooters

There are lots of twisting little lanes and streets in Italy, so many people use small scooters to get around towns and cities.

Leonardo da Vinci

Leonardo da Vinci was one of the world's greatest artists and inventors. In the late 15th century he painted *The Last Supper*, an oil painting showing Jesus Christ's last meal with his apostles (followers).

The Last Supper

Venice

Venice is a city of canals instead of streets. It is built on 118 small islands linked together by bridges. People travel around the city on boats called gondolas.

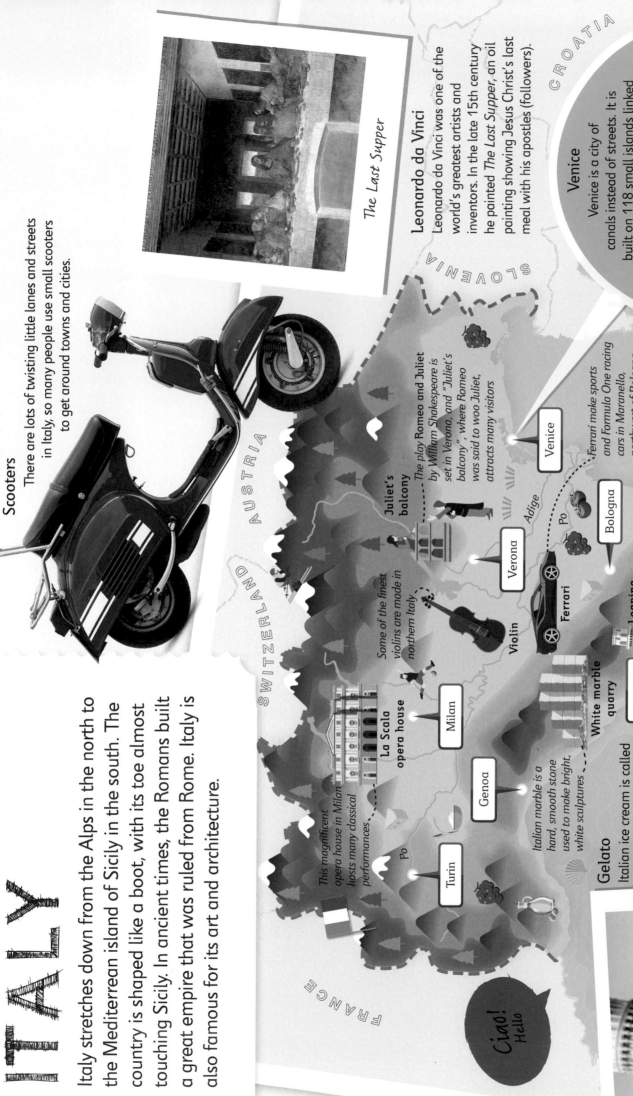

CROATIA

SLOVENIA

AUSTRIA

SWITZERLAND

FRANCE

The play Romeo and Juliet by William Shakespeare is set in Verona, and "Juliet's balcony", where Romeo was said to woo Juliet, attracts many visitors

Juliet's balcony

Venice

Adige

Po

Verona

Ferrari make sports and Formula One racing cars in Maranello, northwest of Bologna

Bologna

Ferrari

SAN MARINO

This tiny independent republic has an area of just over 61 sq km (24 sq miles)

This famous statue in Florence, of the biblical character David, was created by the Italian artist Michelangelo

Michelangelo's sculpture of David

Some of the finest violins are made in northern Italy

Violin

Milan

Leaning Tower of Pisa

Pisa

Arno

Florence

Siena

Tiber

This bell tower tilts to one side because it was built on soft ground

La Scala opera house

This magnificent opera house in Milan hosts many classical performances

Genoa

White marble quarry

Italian marble is a hard, smooth stone used to make bright, white sculptures

Gelato

Italian ice cream is called gelato and is soft and creamy. It comes in lots of delicious flavours, such as vanilla, strawberry, chocolate, and pistachio.

Po

Turin

Ciao! Hello

LIGURIAN SEA

Corsica

Gelato ice cream

N W E S

VATICAN CITY

The Vatican City in Rome is the home of the Pope, the head of the Roman Catholic Church. It is the world's smallest sovereign state

ADRIATIC SEA

These dry stone huts with cone roofs are called trulli and are found in the Italian region of Apulia

Bari

Trulli

This large dormouse is so named because the Ancient Romans ate it as a delicacy

Arrivederci!
Goodbye

Ofanto

Edible dormouse

ITALY

Biferno

Rome

Naples

Mount Vesuvius is a volcano near Naples that erupted in Ancient Roman times, destroying the city of Pompeii. It is still erupting today

Mount Vesuvius

Sicily

Sicily is the largest island in the Mediterranean Sea. Its historic towns and cities, rugged coastline, ancient ruins, and natural wonders, such as the volcano Mount Etna, make it popular with tourists.

Reggio di Calabria

At 3,350 m (10,991 ft), Etna on the island of Sicily is Europe's highest active volcano

Mount Etna

Catania

IONIAN SEA

Colosseum

This large open-air amphitheatre (circular theatre) was built by the Ancient Romans as an arena for gladiator fights. It is the largest amphitheatre ever built.

MEDITERRANEAN SEA

Sicily

Palermo

SCALE

| 0 | 50 miles | 100 miles |

| 0 | 100 kilometres |

Spaghetti is one of hundreds of types of pasta made in Italy, and spaghetti with tomato sauce is a classic dish.

Cagliari

Sardinia

To start the day, Italians drink strong espresso coffee, often made in stove-top coffee pots

Spaghetti

Stove-top coffee pot

Food and drink

Italian food and drink is enjoyed around the world. Italy is the home of the pizza and one of its most popular flavours is the simple margherita pizza made with mozzarella cheese, tomato, and basil.

Margherita pizza

KEY

PRODUCE

Vineyards
Lemons
Olives and oil
Almonds
Figs
Goats
Wheat
Cheese
Rice
Shellfish
Tomatoes

ACTIVITIES

Football
Scuba diving
Skiing
Hiking

INDUSTRY

Fishing

67

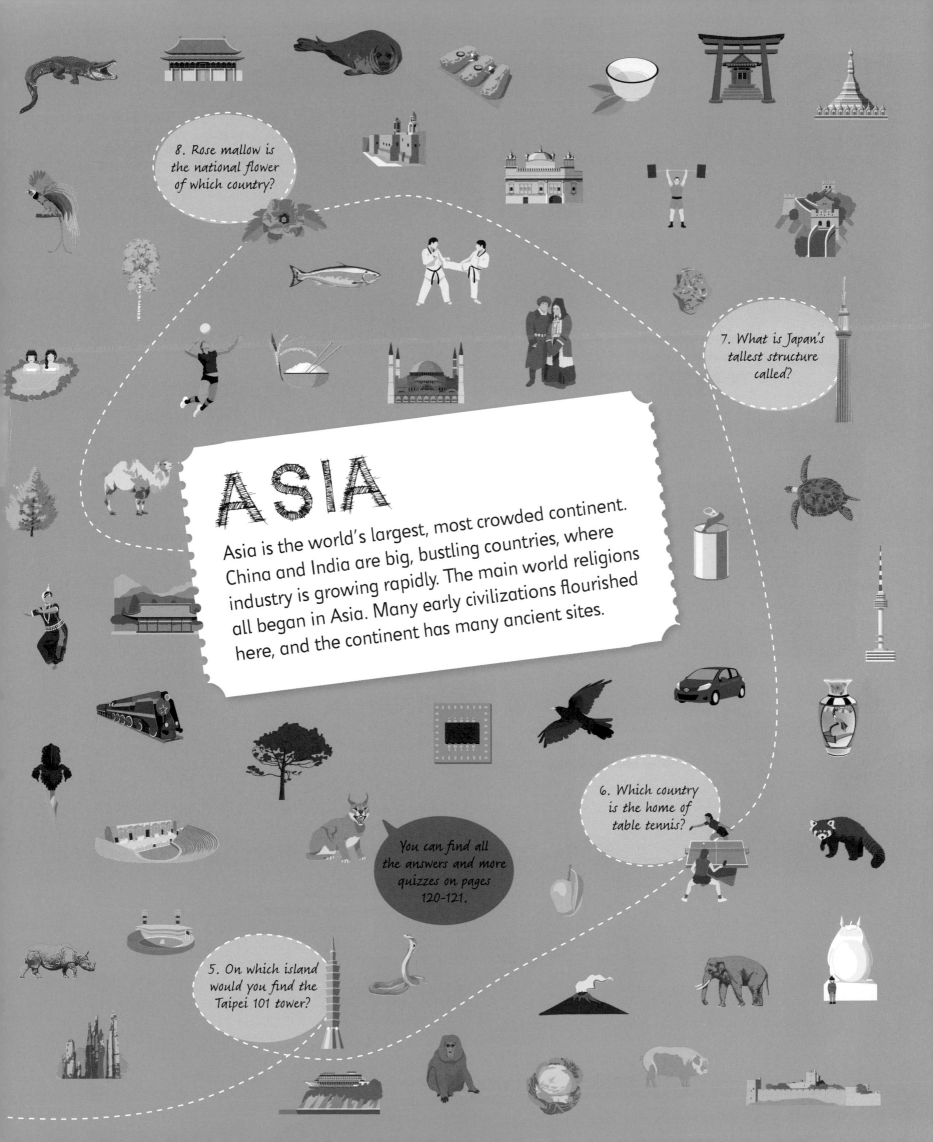

ASIAN RUSSIA AND KAZAKHSTAN

Asian Russia stretches from Europe's border to the Pacific Ocean. Much of the landscape is rugged, with few people living there. Kazakhstan lies to the southwest. This country also has large open spaces, including the vast plains of the Kazakh Steppe.

Presidential Palace
The Akorda Presidential Palace in Astana is the official workplace of the President of Kazakhstan and his staff. This impressive building opened in 2004.

ARCTIC OCEAN

KARA SEA

Hunting with golden eagles
Kazakhs are skilled horse riders. They hunt on horseback on the wide, open plains, using golden eagles to catch prey, such as foxes and hares.

Kazakhs hunting

CASPIAN SEA

RUSSIA (European Russia)

Ural

Yekaterinburg

Sälem! *Hello*

ARCTIC CIRCLE

Noril'sk

Cross-country skiing
This sport is a popular form of exercise during the long winter months

RUSSIA (Asian Russia)

Aktobe

Aktau

KAZAKH STEPPE

Weightlifting is popular in Kazakhstan, with competitions for both men and women

Weightlifting

Irtysh

Ob

These thin, white and silver trees are covered in paper-like bark

Omsk

Novosibirsk

Yenisei

Krasnoyarsk

KEY

PRODUCE
- Wheat
- Sugar beet
- Cattle
- Salmon
- Sheep
- Bactrian camel

SPORT
- Ice hockey

NATURAL FEATURES
- Volcanoes
- Earthquakes

INDUSTRY
- Natural gas
- Oil
- Coal
- Diamonds
- Gold
- Timber
- Aluminium
- Steel
- Iron
- Uranium
- Chromium

ARAL SEA

KAZAKHSTAN

This 97-m (318-ft) tower is the symbol of Astana

Astana

Bayterek Monument

Pavlodar

Silver birch

This antelope has an unusually shaped nose that filters out the dust blowing across the plains in summer

Karaganda

UZBEKISTAN

Shymkent

Lake Balkhash

Saiga antelope

Taraz

Almaty

This Russian Orthodox cathedral is the second tallest wooden building in the world

KYRGYZSTAN

Zenkov Cathedral

CHINA

Hazrat Sultan Mosque
This huge mosque in Kazakhstan's capital, Astana, can hold more than 10,000 worshippers.

SCALE

0 — 600 miles

0 — 600 kilometres

International Space Station
The space station orbits the Earth and was built using Russian technology. Russia's Soyuz spacecraft carries people and supplies to the space station.

Soyuz spacecraft

USA

BERING SEA

LAPTEV SEA

Zdravstvuyte!
Hello

At 4,750 m (15,580 ft), this is the highest, active volcano in Europe and Asia

This small squirrel can glide from tree to tree using the skin stretched between its legs as a parachute

Lena

Klyuchevskaya Sopka

Magadan

Pacific salmon

Siberian flying squirrel

Yakutsk

Yakuts

Yakut people live in the east of Russia. Those near the coast catch fish and look after reindeer, while Yakuts in the south raise cattle and horses

These hot thermal springs naturally heat water to a warming temperature of 40–60°C (104–140°F)

Kamchatka hot springs

Salmon farming
Pacific salmon are farmed off the eastern coast of Russia. They are kept in netted areas of the sea and fed on fishfood pellets and small fish.

This small seal lives only in Lake Baikal

This is the longest railway in the world, stretching 9,300 km (5,780 miles) from Moscow in Europe to the far east of Russia

Amur

Baikal seal

Irkutsk

Khabarovsk

Siberian tiger
The Siberian, or Amur, tiger lives in forests in the far east of Russia. These tigers are rare, and many live in protected conservation areas.

Lake Baikal

YABLONOI MOUNTAINS

Lake Baikal
Lake Baikal is the world's oldest and deepest freshwater lake. The lake is home to more than 1,500 unique species of plants and animals.

MONGOLIA

N
W E
S

Trans-Siberian Railway

CHINA

Vladivostok

TURKEY

Turkey lies partly in Asia and partly in Europe and is influenced by both Eastern and Western culture. Istanbul, the historic city on the Bosphorus river, links the two continents. This huge country has a varied landscape, and its mountains, lakes, beaches, and ancient sites make it attractive to tourists.

Sultan Ahmed Mosque

This mosque in Istanbul is also called the Blue Mosque, because the walls of the interior are covered in light blue tiles. It has six tall minarets, or towers.

Tiles panel, Topkapi Palace

Iznik tiles

These beautiful painted tiles are named after the town where they were made. They decorate the walls of the Topkapi Palace in Istanbul.

Cotton Palace

This unique geological formation is called Pamukkale, or Cotton Palace. It has white limestone terraces, thermal pools, and hot springs, as well as Roman ruins.

BULGARIA

GREECE

Volleyball is a popular sport with both men and women

Volleyball

Bosphorus

These pine trees are important in the Turkish timber industry

Turkish pine

Istanbul

SEA OF MARMARA

Hagia Sophia

Built as a Christian church, Hagia Sophia is now a mosque

Mustafa Kemal Atatürk

Atatürk was the first president of Turkey; he set up his government in Ankara, which replaced Istanbul as the capital in 1923

Bursa

Eskişehir

Ankara

Balıkesir

Merhaba! Hello

TURKEY

İzmir

This ancient Roman building in Ephesus was partly destroyed by an earthquake in 262 CE.

This ancient city was built on hot springs and so had Roman baths as well as an amphitheatre

Lake Tuz

Library of Celsus

Denizli

Hierapolis

Konya

This group of waterfalls flows into the Mediterranean Sea

This stone castle once protected the port of Bodrum

Bodrum Castle

Düden waterfalls

TAURUS MOUNTAINS

Mersin

Antalya

MEDITERRANEAN SEA

CYPRUS

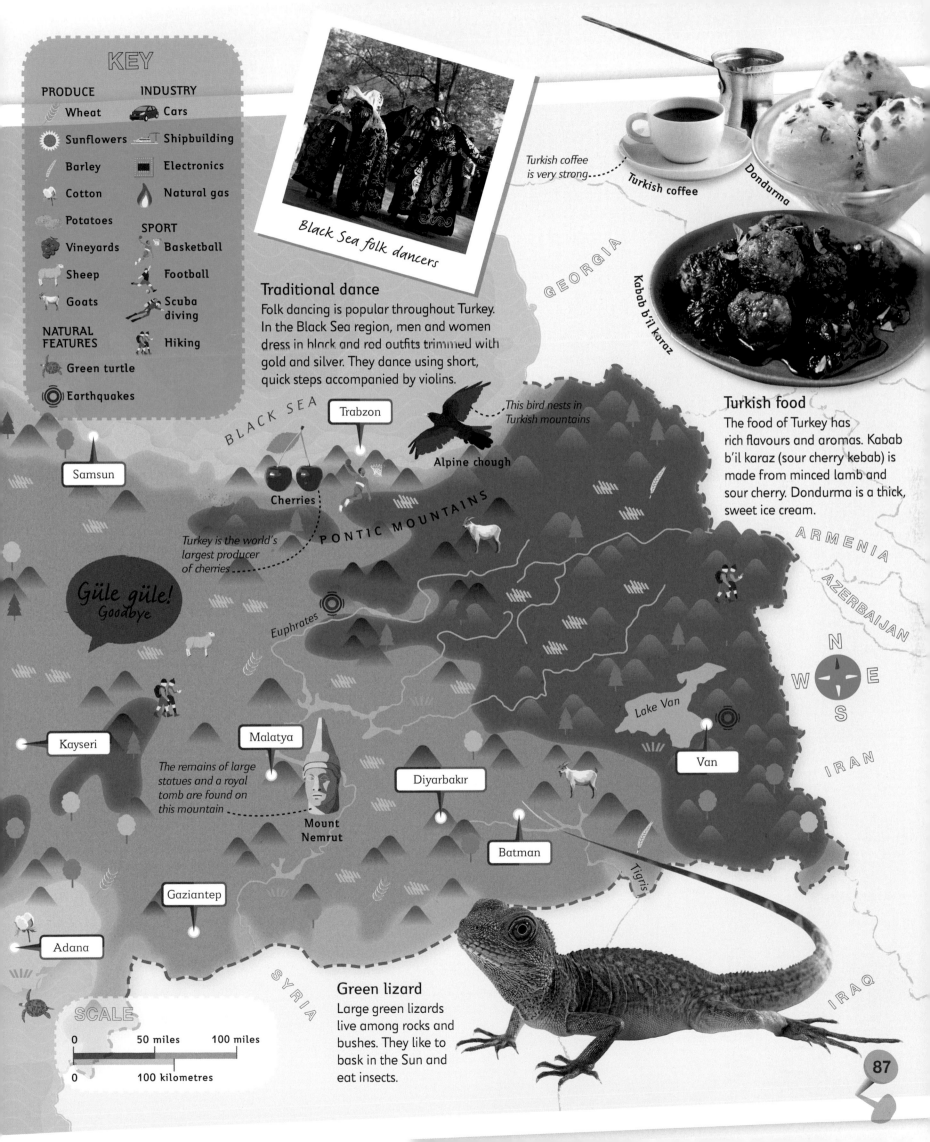

KEY

PRODUCE
- Wheat
- Sunflowers
- Barley
- Cotton
- Potatoes
- Vineyards
- Sheep
- Goats

INDUSTRY
- Cars
- Shipbuilding
- Electronics
- Natural gas

SPORT
- Basketball
- Football
- Scuba diving
- Hiking

NATURAL FEATURES
- Green turtle
- Earthquakes

Black Sea folk dancers

Traditional dance
Folk dancing is popular throughout Turkey. In the Black Sea region, men and women dress in black and red outfits trimmed with gold and silver. They dance using short, quick steps accompanied by violins.

Turkish coffee is very strong

Turkish coffee

Dondurma

Kabab b'il karaz

GEORGIA

Turkish food
The food of Turkey has rich flavours and aromas. Kabab b'il karaz (sour cherry kebab) is made from minced lamb and sour cherry. Dondurma is a thick, sweet ice cream.

ARMENIA

AZERBAIJAN

BLACK SEA

Trabzon

This bird nests in Turkish mountains

Alpine chough

Samsun

Cherries

Turkey is the world's largest producer of cherries

PONTIC MOUNTAINS

Güle güle!
Goodbye

Euphrates

Lake Van

Van

IRAN

N W E S

Kayseri

Malatya

The remains of large statues and a royal tomb are found on this mountain

Diyarbakır

Mount Nemrut

Batman

Tigris

Gaziantep

Adana

SYRIA

IRAQ

Green lizard
Large green lizards live among rocks and bushes. They like to bask in the Sun and eat insects.

SCALE

0   50 miles   100 miles

0   100 kilometres

87

SYRIA AND LEBANON

Syria is largely hot desert, but most people live in the cooler, fertile coastal areas by the Mediterranean Sea. Lebanon lies to the southwest of Syria and has a varied cultural history. The land covered by Syria and Lebanon was once part of the Roman Empire.

Carpet weaving
Beautiful, handwoven carpets are produced in Syria. Their highly detailed, traditional patterns come in a mix of colours, with red and black being particularly popular.

Woman weaving on a loom

KEY

PRODUCE
- Olives
- Vineyards
- Cotton
- Wheat
- Sheep

INDUSTRY
- Oil

TURKEY

Al Hasakah

Manbij

SYRIA

Aleppo

This salad is made from toasted pieces of bread mixed with lettuce and other vegetables

Fattoush salad

These are the only cats that can live in hot deserts. They hunt by night, when it is cooler

Abu Kamal

MEDITERRANEAN SEA

Latakia

Hama

Palmyra

Sand cat

'Ahlaan! Hello

Homs

SYRIAN DESERT

This tree is the national symbol of Lebanon and appears on the country's flag

Tripoli

Cedar of Lebanon

Also known as the Umayyad Mosque, this is one of the oldest and largest mosques in the world

Umayyad dinar

Mortuary statue

Syrian artefacts
Archaeologists have uncovered many ancient artefacts in Syria. These include gold coins, such as Umayyad dinars, and mortuary statues, used to mark graves.

Beirut

Great Mosque of Damascus

Mohammed Al-Amin Mosque

Damascus

LEBANON

This modern mosque has a blue dome and four tall minarets (towers)

IRAQ

JORDAN

ISRAEL

Tyre

Roman ruins at Tyre
The ruins of the Roman city at Tyre in south Lebanon are some of the best-preserved ancient monuments in the world.

Lebanese food
Lebanese food includes delicious snacks such as fatayer, which is a mini pie filled with meat, spinach, or cheese, and light dishes such as tabbouleh, a salad of bulgur wheat, tomatoes, onions, and herbs.

Tabbouleh

Fatayer

Triumphal Arch at Tyre

SCALE
0   50 miles
0   50 kilometres

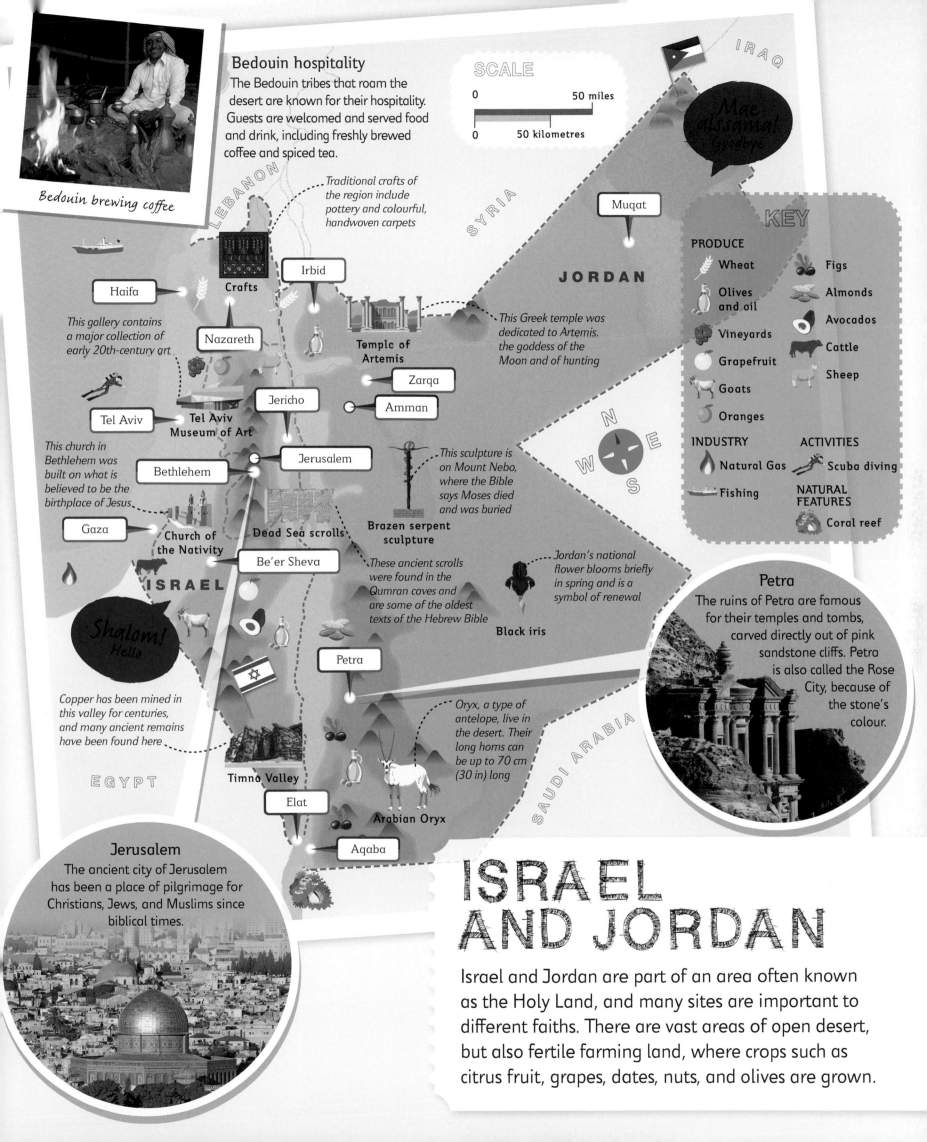

ISRAEL AND JORDAN

Israel and Jordan are part of an area often known as the Holy Land, and many sites are important to different faiths. There are vast areas of open desert, but also fertile farming land, where crops such as citrus fruit, grapes, dates, nuts, and olives are grown.

Bedouin hospitality

The Bedouin tribes that roam the desert are known for their hospitality. Guests are welcomed and served food and drink, including freshly brewed coffee and spiced tea.

Bedouin brewing coffee

SCALE
0 — 50 miles
0 — 50 kilometres

Mae alssama! Goodbye

Traditional crafts of the region include pottery and colourful, handwoven carpets

This gallery contains a major collection of early 20th-century art

This Greek temple was dedicated to Artemis, the goddess of the Moon and of hunting

This church in Bethlehem was built on what is believed to be the birthplace of Jesus

This sculpture is on Mount Nebo, where the Bible says Moses died and was buried

These ancient scrolls were found in the Qumran caves and are some of the oldest texts of the Hebrew Bible

Jordan's national flower blooms briefly in spring and is a symbol of renewal

Shalom! Hello

Copper has been mined in this valley for centuries, and many ancient remains have been found here

Oryx, a type of antelope, live in the desert. Their long horns can be up to 70 cm (30 in) long

KEY

PRODUCE
- Wheat
- Olives and oil
- Vineyards
- Grapefruit
- Goats
- Oranges
- Figs
- Almonds
- Avocados
- Cattle
- Sheep

INDUSTRY
- Natural Gas
- Fishing

ACTIVITIES
- Scuba diving

NATURAL FEATURES
- Coral reef

Petra

The ruins of Petra are famous for their temples and tombs, carved directly out of pink sandstone cliffs. Petra is also called the Rose City, because of the stone's colour.

Jerusalem

The ancient city of Jerusalem has been a place of pilgrimage for Christians, Jews, and Muslims since biblical times.

Labels: IRAQ, SYRIA, LEBANON, JORDAN, ISRAEL, EGYPT, SAUDI ARABIA, Muqat, Irbid, Haifa, Crafts, Nazareth, Temple of Artemis, Zarqa, Amman, Jericho, Tel Aviv, Tel Aviv Museum of Art, Jerusalem, Bethlehem, Church of the Nativity, Gaza, Dead Sea scrolls, Brazen serpent sculpture, Be'er Sheva, Black iris, Petra, Timna Valley, Arabian Oryx, Elat, Aqaba

IRAN, IRAQ, AND SAUDI ARABIA

Iran, Iraq, and Saudi Arabia all contain large areas of hot, sandy desert, with huge reserves of oil and natural gas. Some of the world's earliest civilizations flourished in these lands, and all three countries have many ancient ruins and other treasures.

Fine foods

This region is noted for producing some of the world's most prized delicacies. These include high-quality dates, the delicate spice saffron, and the best and most expensive caviar (fish eggs).

Dates

Saffron

Caviar

Colourful tiles

The Safavid Empire ruled Persia (modern-day Iran) from the 14th to the 18th century. The capital of this empire was Isfahan, which was known for its fine art, including colourful tiles.

Isfahan tile

Ur treasure

Ur was an important ancient city in what is now Iraq. Many treasures were found in tombs there. These include intricate gold jewellery and a lyre (type of harp) decorated with a golden bull's head.

Bull's head lyre

Gold wreath

Queen's jewellery

Map labels

TURKMENISTAN

AFGHANISTAN

Dorood!
Hello

IRAN

Mashhad

Turquoise
This gemstone has been mined in Iran for more than 5,000 years

LUT DESERT

Backgammon
This board game has been played in Iraq and Iran for centuries

Zahedan

KAVIR DESERT

Pigeon Tower
Dung collected from these Safavid "homes" for pigeons was used as fertilizer

The ruins of the Persian city of Persepolis date back to 515 BCE

Shiraz

Persepolis ruins

Isfahan
This 17th-century Isfahan mosque is one of the most beautiful in Iran

CASPIAN SEA

Eggs from this large fish are made into caviar

Beluga sturgeon

ELBURZ MOUNTAINS

Tehran

Imam Mosque

ZAGROS MOUNTAINS

Ahvaz

Basra

Tabriz

Kirkuk

KUWAIT

Erbil

Ziggurat of Ur

Marsh Arab reed building

TURKEY

Mosul

Baghdad

Najaf

IRAQ

SYRIA

Salam alaikum!
Hello

This ancient temple stood near the city of Ur

Marsh Arabs live in the wetlands of south and east Iraq and build houses using reeds

Al Jawf

The tombs carved into the rocks here date from the 1st century CE

The Bedouin people live in tents in the desert

JORDAN

Bedouin tent

Mada'in Saleh

ARABIAN DESERT

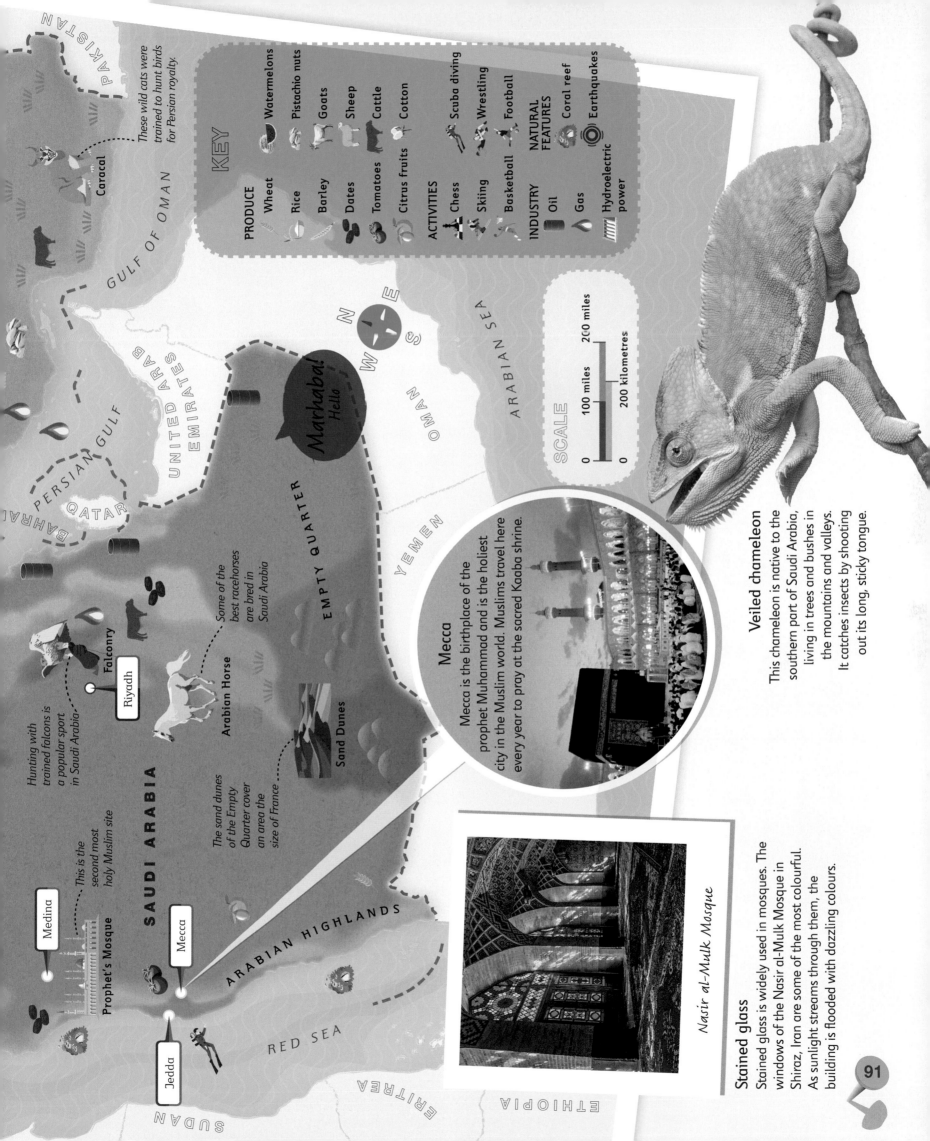

KEY

PRODUCE
- 🍉 Watermelons
- Wheat
- Pistachio nuts
- Rice
- Goats
- Barley
- Sheep
- Dates
- Cattle
- Tomatoes
- Cotton
- Citrus fruits

ACTIVITIES
- Scuba diving
- Chess
- Wrestling
- Skiing
- Football
- Basketball

INDUSTRY
- Oil
- Scuba diving
- Gas
- Coral reef

NATURAL FEATURES
- Coral reef
- Earthquakes
- Hydroelectric power

These wild cats were trained to hunt birds for Persian royalty.

Caracal

PAKISTAN

GULF OF OMAN

UNITED ARAB EMIRATES

PERSIAN GULF

QATAR

BAHRAIN

Marhaba!
Hello

N W E S

OMAN

YEMEN

ARABIAN SEA

SCALE

0 ___ 100 miles ___ 200 miles
0 ___ 200 kilometres

Hunting with trained falcons is a popular sport in Saudi Arabia.

Falconry

Riyadh

Some of the best racehorses are bred in Saudi Arabia

Arabian Horse

EMPTY QUARTER

The sand dunes of the Empty Quarter cover an area the size of France

Sand Dunes

SAUDI ARABIA

This is the second most holy Muslim site

Medina

Prophet's Mosque

Mecca

ARABIAN HIGHLANDS

Jedda

RED SEA

SUDAN

ERITREA

ETHIOPIA

Mecca

Mecca is the birthplace of the prophet Muhammad and is the holiest city in the Muslim world. Muslims travel here every year to pray at the sacred Kaaba shrine.

Nasir al-Mulk Mosque

Stained glass

Stained glass is widely used in mosques. The windows of the Nasir al-Mulk Mosque in Shiraz, Iran are some of the most colourful. As sunlight streams through them, the building is flooded with dazzling colours.

Veiled chameleon

This chameleon is native to the southern part of Saudi Arabia, living in trees and bushes in the mountains and valleys. It catches insects by shooting out its long, sticky tongue.

AFGHANISTAN

Afghanistan lies between Central Asia and China. In ancient times, Chinese silk and other goods were traded along the Silk Road that passed through the Hindu Kush mountains. Temperatures in the deserts and mountains of Afghanistan vary from very hot in summer to freezing cold in winter.

Band-e Amir lakes
Six deep lakes lie side by side at Band-e Amir, in the Hindu Kush mountains. They are part of Afghanistan's first national park.

These unusual sheep have huge, spiralling horns, which can be up to 70 cm (27 in) long

Marco Polo sheep

This highly prized gemstone has been mined in Afghanistan for over 5,000 years

Lapis lazuli

Pistachios

Apricots

Pomegranates

Fruit and nuts
Afghanistan's farms produce some of the tastiest nuts and fruit in the world. These include large quantities of pistachio nuts, apricots, and pomegranates.

Citadel of Herat
This huge castle has 18 towers and 2-m (6½-ft) thick brick walls. It stands on the site of a fort built by Alexander the Great in 330 BCE.

TURKMENISTAN

UZBEKISTAN

TAJIKISTAN

CHINA

Mazar-i-Sharif

HINDU KUSH

Ancient Buddhist statues and manuscripts were discovered in these caves

Pistachio trees grow wild in many parts of Afghanistan

Bamiyan

Jalalabad

Bamiyan caves

Kabul

Khyber Pass
This mountain pass links Afghanistan with Pakistan

IRAN

Hari Rud

Herat

Pistachio tree

This large mosque in Herat is covered in beautiful glazed tiles

Jama Masjid

Afghan rug

Afghan rugs are prized all over the world

PAKISTAN

Bactrian gold
This hoard of gold artefacts was discovered in ancient burial mounds in northern Afghanistan in 1978. It includes jewellery, coins, and figures.

Farah Rud

Kandahar

REGISTAN DESERT

Helmand

Embroidered hat
Traditional clothes in Afghanistan have colourful, detailed embroidery, such as on this child's hat.

SCALE
0 — 100 miles
0 — 100 kilometres

Salaam!
Hello

KEY

PRODUCE
- Wheat
- Maize
- Barley
- Rice
- Potatoes
- Raisins
- Apricots
- Cotton
- Sheep
- Goats
- Pomegranates

ACTIVITIES
- Basketball
- Football
- Cricket

NATURAL FEATURES
- Sapphires
- Earthquakes

PAKISTAN

Pakistan has the world's fifth largest population. Many people live along the Indus river and its tributaries (streams), which flow down through the middle of the country, providing water to irrigate the fertile farmland along the riverbanks. Farming is Pakistan's main source of income.

Snow leopards live in Pakistan's northern mountains, which include K2, the world's second highest mountain

K 2

CHINA

HINDU KUSH

KARAKORUM RANGE

Snow leopard

Markhor
This large mountain goat is the national animal of Pakistan. Males are prized for their long, corkscrew-like horns.

Islamabad

This 148-m (485-ft) high dam generates hydroelectric power

AFGHANISTAN

Tarbela Dam

Peshawar

Rawalpindi

Gujranwala

INDIA

Lahore

Badshahi Mosque

Faisal Mosque
This modern mosque is in the capital, Islamabad. It is Pakistan's largest mosque and its distinctive design is in the shape of a Bedouin tent.

Over 100,000 people can pray together at this mosque in Lahore

This is Pakistan's national flower; it has a rich perfume

Poet's jasmine

Faisalabad

Salaam!
Hello

Multan

Many people work in the textile industry in Pakistan

This tasty fish is a popular source of food

Derawar Fort

The 40 towers of this large fort can be seen from great distances across the desert

SCALE
0 ——— 100 miles

0 ——— 100 kilometres

N W E S

Textiles

Rita catfish

THAR DESERT

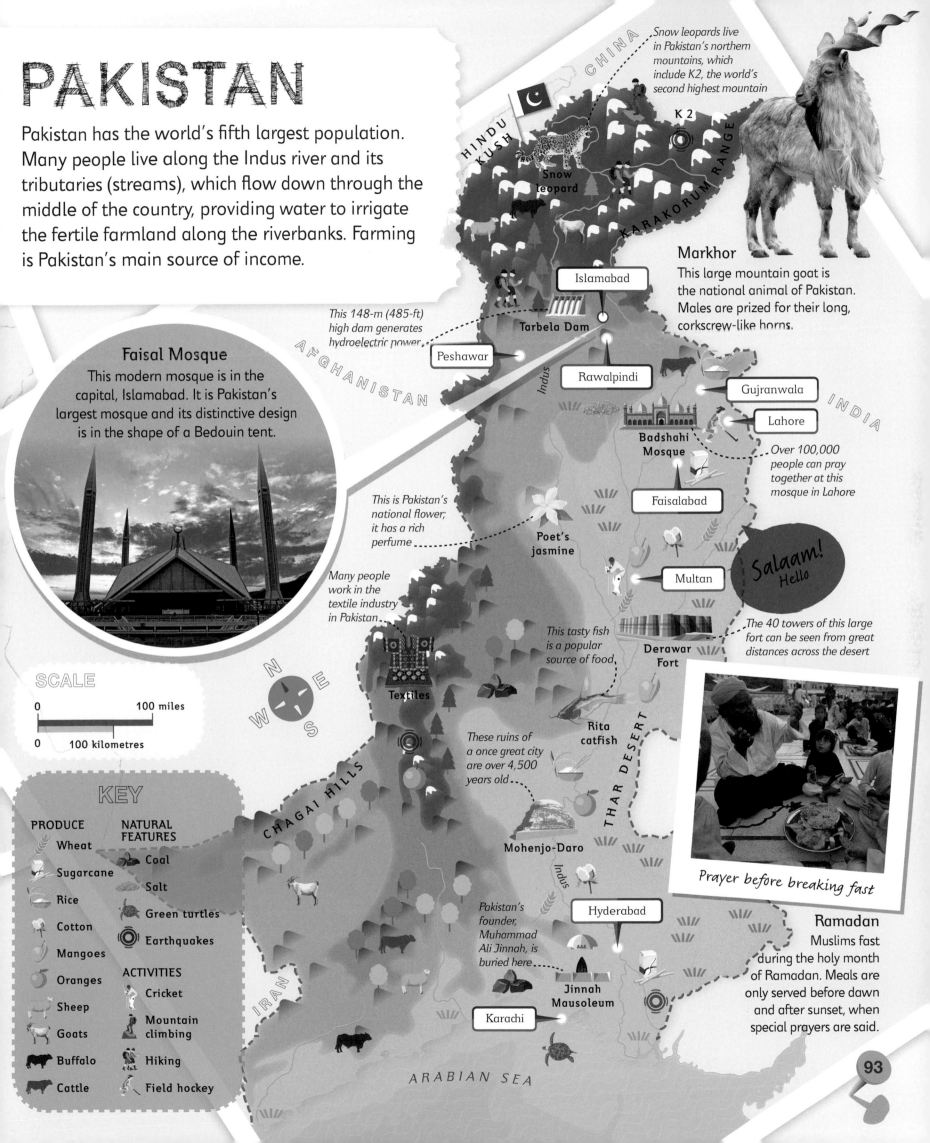

Prayer before breaking fast

CHAGAI HILLS

These ruins of a once great city are over 4,500 years old

Mohenjo-Daro

Indus

KEY

PRODUCE
- Wheat
- Sugarcane
- Rice
- Cotton
- Mangoes
- Oranges
- Sheep
- Goats
- Buffalo
- Cattle

NATURAL FEATURES
- Coal
- Salt
- Green turtles
- Earthquakes

ACTIVITIES
- Cricket
- Mountain climbing
- Hiking
- Field hockey

Pakistan's founder, Muhammad Ali Jinnah, is buried here

Hyderabad

Ramadan
Muslims fast during the holy month of Ramadan. Meals are only served before dawn and after sunset, when special prayers are said.

IRAN

Jinnah Mausoleum

Karachi

ARABIAN SEA

INDIA AND SRI LANKA

India is a colourful and crowded country. It stretches from the snowy Himalayan mountains to the warm waters of the Indian Ocean. Sri Lanka is a tropical island that is known for its tea plantations.

Land of spices

Rich and fragrant spices are grown in India and Sri Lanka. The ginger root adds warmth to sweet and savoury dishes and several different spices are used in curries.

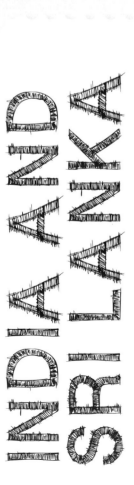

Ginger

Selection of spices

Cricket

Cricket is the most popular sport in India. It is played across the country on grass cricket grounds like this one in the city of Mumbai.

Cricketers in Mumbai

Holi Festival

The Hindu spring festival celebrates colour and love. People throw paint powder and get covered in bright colours.

Throwing coloured paint

Peacock

The peacock is the national bird of India. The males have amazing tail feathers with swirled patterns that look like eyes.

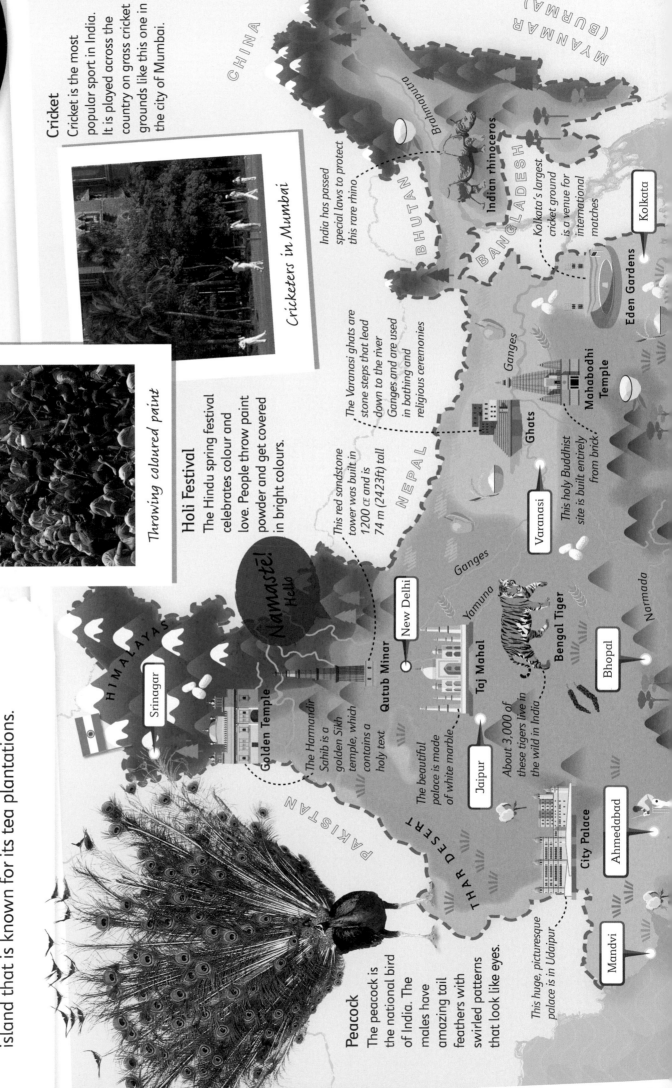

CHINA

MYANMAR (BURMA)

BHUTAN

Brahmaputra

Indian rhinoceros

India has passed special laws to protect this rare rhino

BANGLADESH

Kolkata's largest cricket ground is a venue for international matches

Kolkata

Eden Gardens

Ganges

The Varanasi ghats are stone steps that lead down to the river Ganges and are used in bathing and religious ceremonies

Ghats

Mahabodhi Temple

This holy Buddhist site is built entirely from brick

Varanasi

NEPAL

This red sandstone tower was built in 1200 CE and is 74 m (2423ft) tall

Namaste! Hello

Ganges

Yamuna

New Delhi

Qutub Minar

Bengal Tiger

Narmada

HIMALAYAS

Srinagar

Golden Temple

The Harmandir Sahib is a golden Sikh temple, which contains a holy text

Taj Mahal

The beautiful palace is made of white marble.

Jaipur

About 3,000 of these tigers live in the wild in India

Bhopal

PAKISTAN

THAR DESERT

City Palace

Ahmedabad

This huge, picturesque palace is in Udaipur

Mandvi

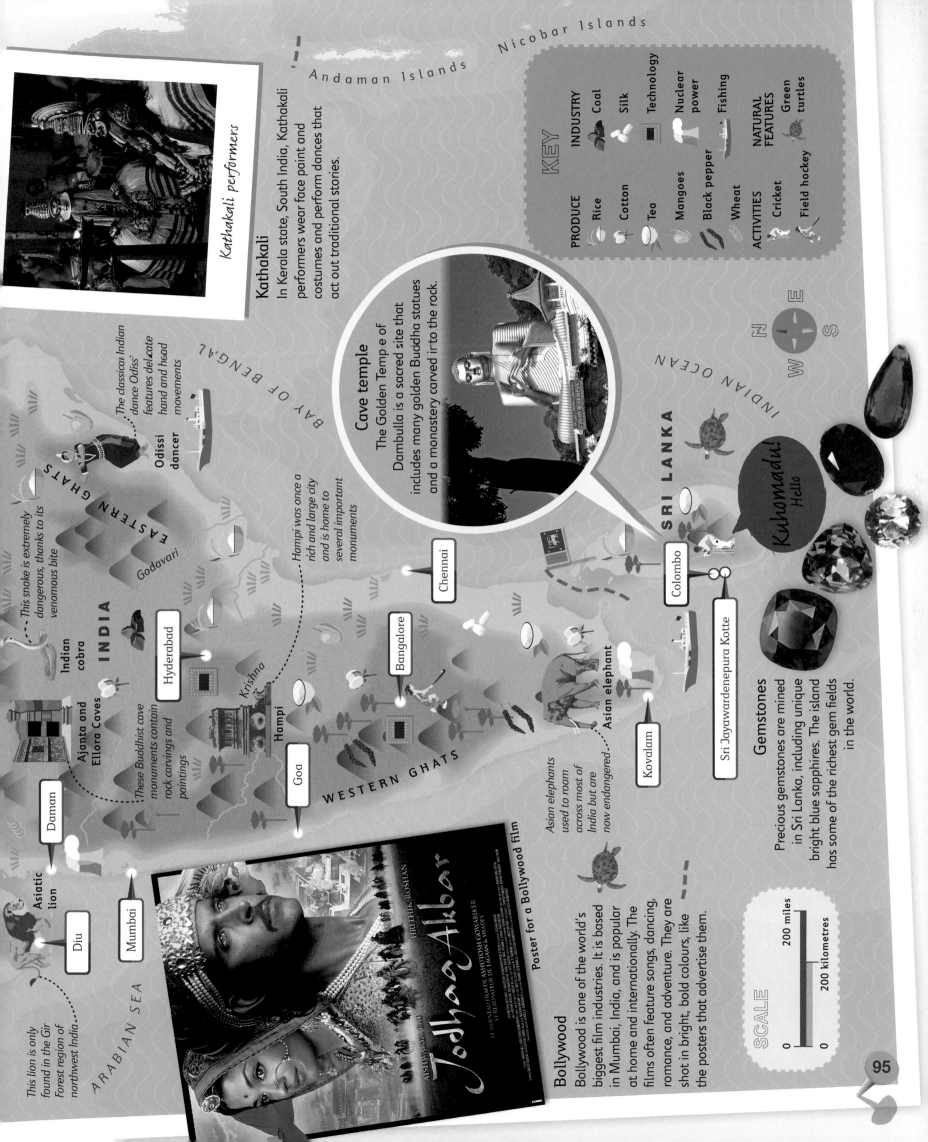

Kathakali performers

Kathakali

In Kerala state, South India, Kathakali performers wear face paint and costumes and perform dances that act out traditional stories.

Nicobar Islands

Andaman Islands

KEY

INDUSTRY
- Coal
- Silk
- Technology
- Nuclear power
- Fishing

NATURAL FEATURES
- Green turtles

PRODUCE
- Rice
- Cotton
- Tea
- Mangoes
- Black pepper
- Wheat

ACTIVITIES
- Cricket
- Field hockey

BAY OF BENGAL

The classical Indian dance Odissi features delicate hand and head movements

Odissi dancer

EASTERN GHATS

This snake is extremely dangerous, thanks to its venomous bite

Indian cobra

INDIA

Godavari

Hampi was once a rich and large city and is home to several important monuments

Cave temple

The Golden Temple of Dambulla is a sacred site that includes many golden Buddha statues and a monastery carved into the rock.

These Buddhist cave monuments contain rock carvings and paintings

Ajanta and Ellora Caves

Hyderabad

Krishna

Hampi

Chennai

Bangalore

Goa

WESTERN GHATS

Asian elephants used to roam across most of India but are now endangered

Asian elephant

Kovalam

Daman

Asiatic lion

This lion is only found in the Gir Forest region of northwest India

Diu

Mumbai

ARABIAN SEA

SRI LANKA

Kuhomadu!
Hello

Colombo

Sri Jayawardenepura Kotte

INDIAN OCEAN

N
W E
S

Gemstones

Precious gemstones are mined in Sri Lanka, including unique bright blue sapphires. The island has some of the richest gem fields in the world.

Bollywood

Bollywood is one of the world's biggest film industries. It is based in Mumbai, India, and is popular at home and internationally. The films often feature songs, dancing, romance, and adventure. They are shot in bright, bold colours, like the posters that advertise them.

Poster for a Bollywood film

SCALE

0 — 200 miles

0 — 200 kilometres

95

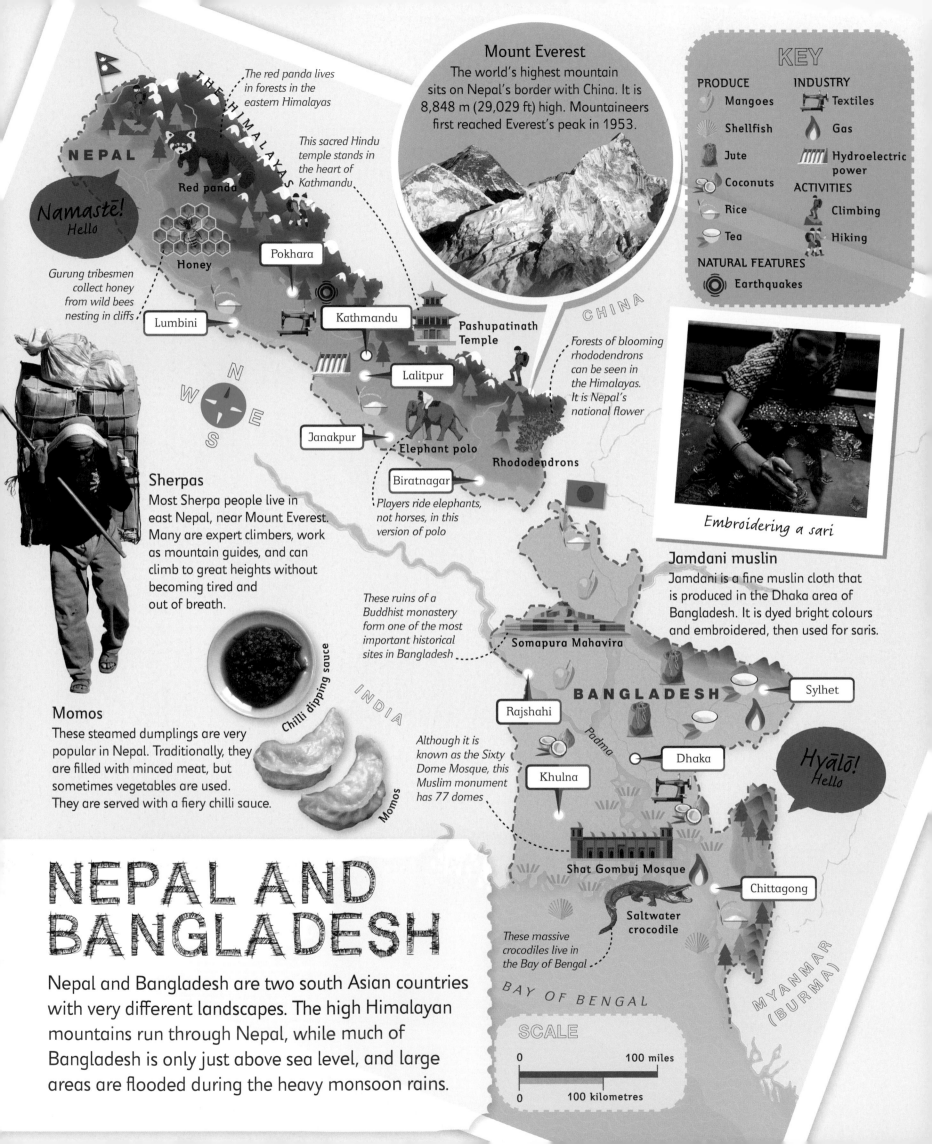

The red panda lives in forests in the eastern Himalayas

THE HIMALAYAS

NEPAL

Red panda

Namastē! Hello

This sacred Hindu temple stands in the heart of Kathmandu

Mount Everest
The world's highest mountain sits on Nepal's border with China. It is 8,848 m (29,029 ft) high. Mountaineers first reached Everest's peak in 1953.

KEY
PRODUCE
- Mangoes
- Shellfish
- Jute
- Coconuts
- Rice
- Tea

INDUSTRY
- Textiles
- Gas
- Hydroelectric power

ACTIVITIES
- Climbing
- Hiking

NATURAL FEATURES
- Earthquakes

Gurung tribesmen collect honey from wild bees nesting in cliffs

Honey

Pokhara

Lumbini

Kathmandu

Pashupatinath Temple

CHINA

Lalitpur

Forests of blooming rhododendrons can be seen in the Himalayas. It is Nepal's national flower

Janakpur

Elephant polo

Rhododendrons

Embroidering a sari

Biratnagar

Players ride elephants, not horses, in this version of polo

Sherpas
Most Sherpa people live in east Nepal, near Mount Everest. Many are expert climbers, work as mountain guides, and can climb to great heights without becoming tired and out of breath.

Jamdani muslin
Jamdani is a fine muslin cloth that is produced in the Dhaka area of Bangladesh. It is dyed bright colours and embroidered, then used for saris.

These ruins of a Buddhist monastery form one of the most important historical sites in Bangladesh

Somapura Mahavira

Chilli dipping sauce

INDIA

Momos
These steamed dumplings are very popular in Nepal. Traditionally, they are filled with minced meat, but sometimes vegetables are used. They are served with a fiery chilli sauce.

Momos

BANGLADESH

Rajshahi

Sylhet

Although it is known as the Sixty Dome Mosque, this Muslim monument has 77 domes

Padma

Dhaka

Khulna

Hyālō! Hello

Shat Gombuj Mosque

Saltwater crocodile

Chittagong

These massive crocodiles live in the Bay of Bengal

NEPAL AND BANGLADESH

Nepal and Bangladesh are two south Asian countries with very different landscapes. The high Himalayan mountains run through Nepal, while much of Bangladesh is only just above sea level, and large areas are flooded during the heavy monsoon rains.

BAY OF BENGAL

MYANMAR (BURMA)

SCALE
0 — 100 miles
0 — 100 kilometres

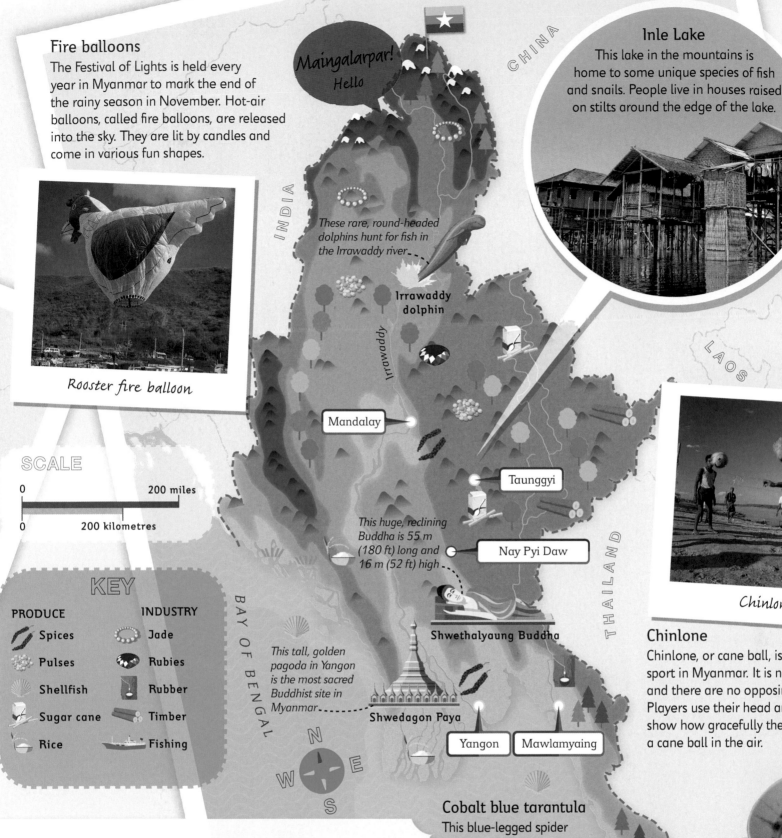

Fire balloons

The Festival of Lights is held every year in Myanmar to mark the end of the rainy season in November. Hot-air balloons, called fire balloons, are released into the sky. They are lit by candles and come in various fun shapes.

Maingalarpar!
Hello

Rooster fire balloon

CHINA

INDIA

These rare, round-headed dolphins hunt for fish in the Irrawaddy river

Irrawaddy dolphin

Irrawaddy

Inle Lake

This lake in the mountains is home to some unique species of fish and snails. People live in houses raised on stilts around the edge of the lake.

LAOS

Mandalay

Taunggyi

This huge, reclining Buddha is 55 m (180 ft) long and 16 m (52 ft) high

Nay Pyi Daw

THAILAND

Chinlone

SCALE

0 ————— 200 miles

0 ————— 200 kilometres

KEY

PRODUCE

- Spices
- Pulses
- Shellfish
- Sugar cane
- Rice

INDUSTRY

- Jade
- Rubies
- Rubber
- Timber
- Fishing

BAY OF BENGAL

This tall, golden pagoda in Yangon is the most sacred Buddhist site in Myanmar

Shwethalyaung Buddha

Shwedagon Paya

Yangon   Mawlamyaing

N W E S

Chinlone

Chinlone, or cane ball, is a traditional sport in Myanmar. It is not competitive and there are no opposing teams. Players use their head and knees to show how gracefully they can keep a cane ball in the air.

Cobalt blue tarantula

This blue-legged spider lives in Myanmar's tropical forests. It uses deadly venom to catch its prey, including mice and frogs.

Shan noodles

This popular dish uses flat rice noodles, which are served in a spicy broth with chicken or pork. It is served topped with mustard greens and chopped peanuts.

MYANMAR

Myanmar (formerly Burma) is a long, thin country that follows the Irrawaddy River and the coast of the Bay of Bengal. In the hills and forests of Myanmar, there are mines containing precious gemstones, such as jade and rubies. Its forests produce some of the world's finest teak wood, which is very hardwearing and is used in shipbuilding and to make furniture.

CHINA AND MONGOLIA

More than 1 billion people live in China. Most people live in the industrialized east of this vast and ancient land, which was once the home of a great empire. Mongolia has far fewer people and much of the country is desert or grassland, called steppe.

Baby dinosaur fossils

Dinosaurs in the Gobi
Dinosaurs lived in Mongolia and China millions of years ago. Many well-preserved dinosaur fossils have been found in the Gobi desert.

MONGOLIA

People use this two-humped camel to carry goods in the Gobi desert

KAZAKHSTAN

KYRGYZSTAN

Ni hǎo!
Hello

Sain uu!
Hello

TAJIKISTAN

TAKLAMAKAN DESERT

Bactrian camel

PAKISTAN

Tibetan monk

Buddhism
Buddhism is a religion and a philosophy based on the teachings of the Buddha. In Tibet, Buddhist monks wear red robes.

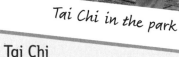
Tai Chi in the park

Tai Chi
This popular group exercise involves a series of slow, controlled movements. People practise Tai Chi for defensive training and to keep healthy.

Yak are kept for their milk, meat, and wool, and for transport

Yak

PLATEAU OF TIBET

HIMALAYAS

Lhasa

NEPAL

Potala Palace

This Tibetan palace was the home of the Dalai Lama, the spiritual head of Tibetan Buddhism

BHUTAN

INDIA

MYANMAR (BURMA)

Giant panda
The giant panda lives in the mountainous forests of south-central China. It feeds on bamboo and is one of the rarest animals in the world.

Chinese New Year
This is China's most important festival, when people celebrate the coming of spring. People hold parades led by a huge dancing dragon, a symbol of China that is believed to bring good luck.

Mongolian horses
There are more horses in Mongolia than people. The Mongol horse is small, but very strong and sturdy. Many children learn to ride by the age of three.

RUSSIA

Porcelain
China is famous for its high-quality, hardwearing pottery, called porcelain, which is made from kaolin, also known as China Clay.

Ulan Bator

Harbin

Many Mongolians live in ghers, which are large, round portable tents covered in animal skins

Mongolian gher

This Chinese imperial palace was once the home of the emperor

GOBI DESERT

Shenyang

NORTH KOREA

Forbidden City

Beijing

China built the Great Wall to protect the country from invaders

This popular indoor sport is also known as ping-pong

Tianjin

Great Wall of China

CHINA

Table tennis

Yellow River

YELLOW SEA

Chinese food
Chinese cuisine is known for its variety of flavours. Meals often include rice or noodles and are eaten with chopsticks. Dim sum is a traditional Chinese food that consists of small bite-sized portions

Dim sum

Chopsticks

Rice

The world's tallest type of grass can grow as high as a tree

These sculptures, found in the ancient capital of Xi'an, were made for the emperor to protect him in the afterlife

Nanjing

EAST CHINA SEA

Xi'an

Terracotta Army

This park features dramatic sandstone pillars and peaks

Wuhan

Shanghai

Hangzhou

Taroko Gorge
The Leehow River carved through marble rock near Taiwan's east coast, creating this gorge, which is also called Marble Gorge.

Bamboo

Chengdu

Jingdezhen

Chongqing

Yangtze

Wulingyuan National Park

Native to China, this tree is used in Chinese medicine

This skyscraper in Tapei was designed to look like a bamboo stalk

Golden larch

More than 1 million people visit Guilin every year to see its stunning landscape

Taipei

Taipei 101

This dolphin lives in coastal areas and rivers

TAIWAN

Hong Kong
This region of China has a deep natural harbour and a dynamic skyline filled with tall skyscrapers. It is one of the most crowded areas in the world.

Pearl River

Guilin

Guangzhou

Hong Kong

Indo-Pacific humpback dolphin

VIETNAM

LAOS

Hainan

SCALE

0   200 miles

0   200 kilometres

N W S E

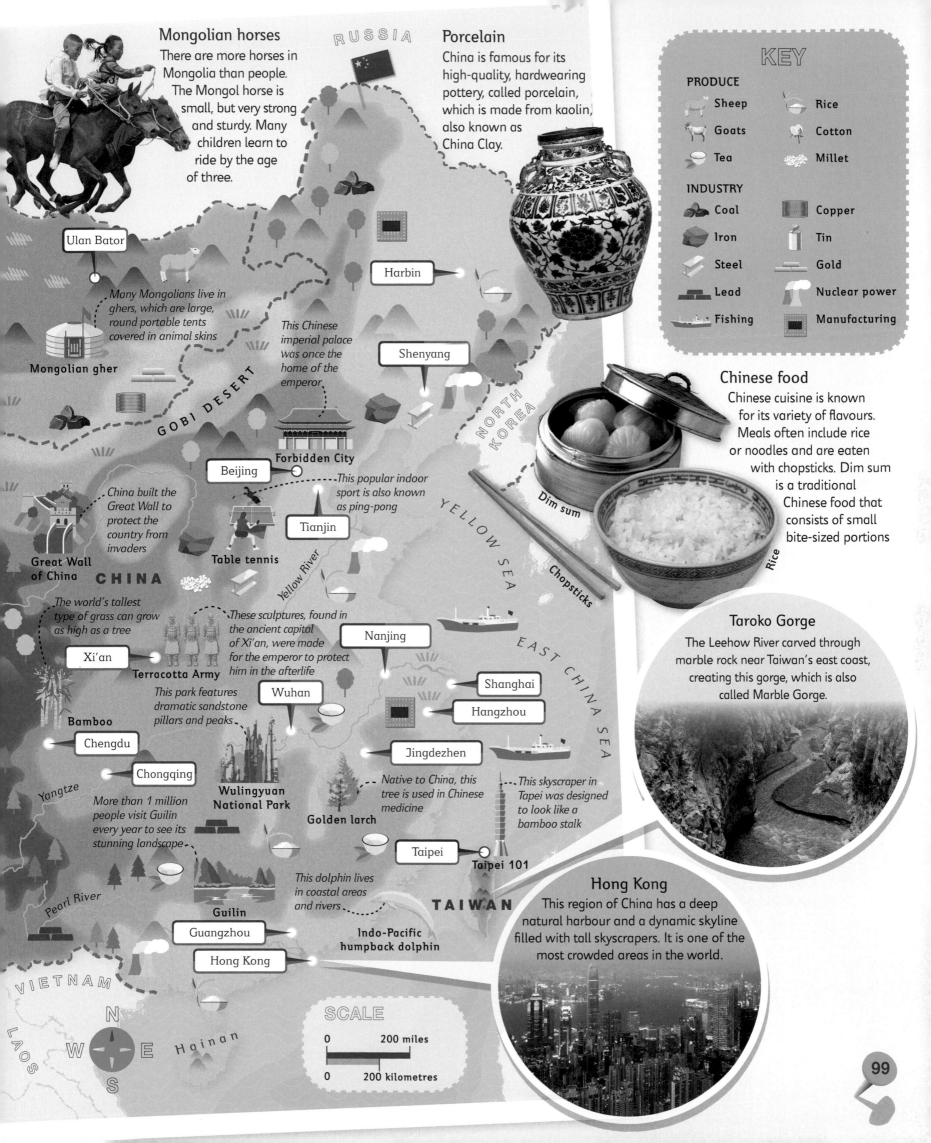

KOREA

Korea is a long peninsula that is divided into two countries: North Korea and South Korea, which are very different from each other. North Korea is mountainous and rural. Its society is ordered and closed off from the world. South Korea is more modern and has a thriving electronics industry.

RUSSIA

CHINA

NORTH KOREA

SEA OF JAPAN/EAST SEA

KOREA BAY

Sacred mountain
Mount Paektu is Korea's highest mountain and is sacred to the Korean people. It is also an active volcano and has a large lake at the top.

Fruit and vegetables
The Asian pear is native to Korea and is commonly found in gardens. The pear has a yellow skin and a crisp texture. Chinese cabbage, a green-leaf vegetable, is grown in Korea.

Chinese cabbage

Asian pear

This animal fattens up for the cold Korean winter by eating birds, frogs, and fruit

Raccoon dog

Annyeonghi gaseyo!
Goodbye

Chongjin

The internet
South Korea has the fastest internet connection rate in the world. Everyone uses the internet for work, school, and play. Many Korean teenagers enjoy playing games online.

Using the internet

SCALE

| 0 | | 50 miles |
| 0 | | 50 kilometres |

This beautiful mountain features in many Korean works of art

Mount Kumgang

Hamhung

This mountain is a sacred site and major tourist attraction

Myohyang-san

Wonsan

This 150-m (492-ft) high monument has a metal torch at the top, which is lit up at night

Juche Tower

Taedong

Kumsusan Palace of the Sun
This palace in Pyongyang is a mausoleum (burial chamber) that contains the body of Kim Il-sung, the founding president of North Korea.

Pyongyang

Sinuiju

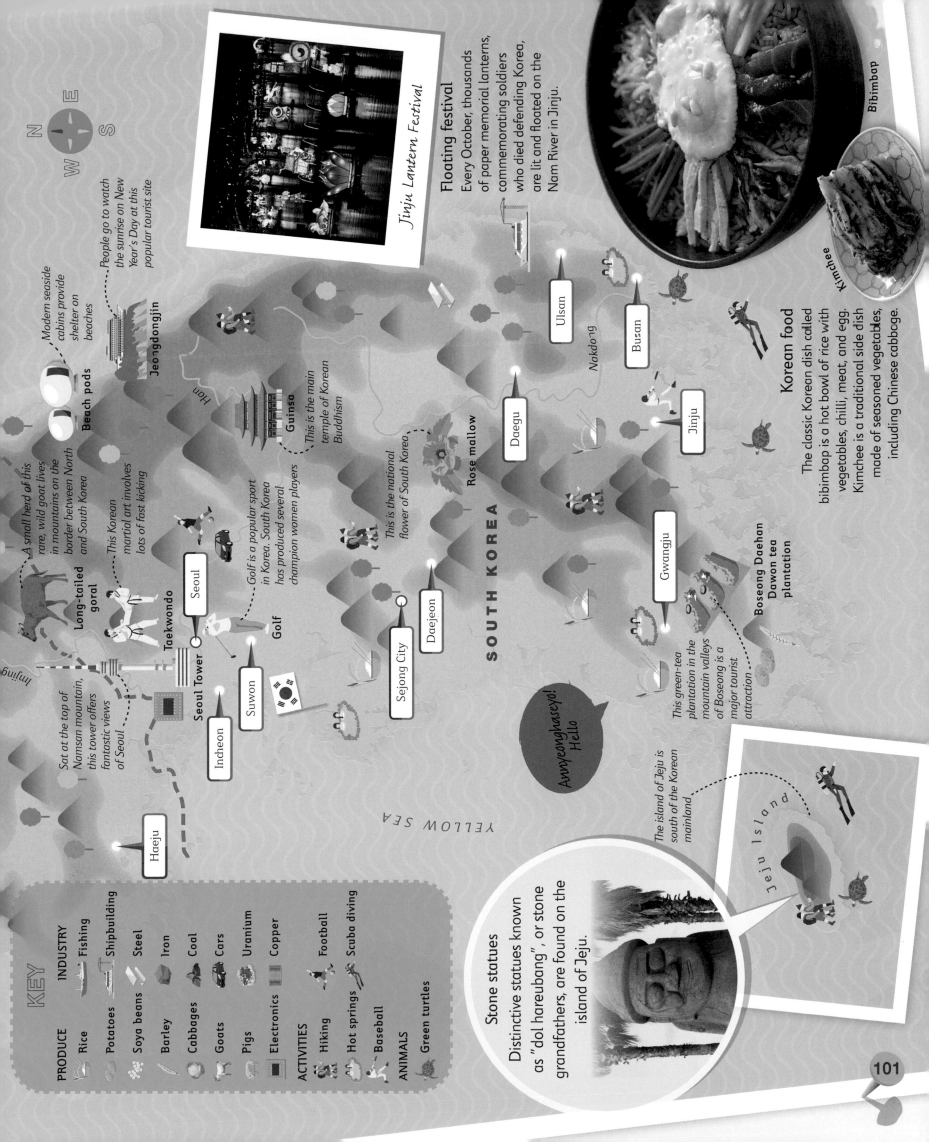

KEY

PRODUCE
- Rice
- Potatoes
- Soya beans
- Barley
- Cabbages
- Goats
- Pigs
- Electronics

INDUSTRY
- Fishing
- Shipbuilding
- Steel
- Iron
- Coal
- Cars
- Uranium
- Copper

ACTIVITIES
- Hiking
- Hot springs
- Baseball
- Football
- Scuba diving

ANIMALS
- Green turtles

Jinju Lantern Festival

Floating festival
Every October, thousands of paper memorial lanterns, commemorating soldiers who died defending Korea, are lit and floated on the Nam River in Jinju.

Korean food
The classic Korean dish called bibimbap is a hot bowl of rice with vegetables, chilli, meat, and egg. Kimchee is a traditional side dish made of seasoned vegetables, including Chinese cabbage.

Bibimbap

Kimchee

People go to watch the sunrise on New Year's Day at this popular tourist site

Modern seaside cabins provide shelter on beaches

Beach pods

Jeongdongjin

A small herd of this rare, wild goat lives in mountains on the border between North and South Korea

Long-tailed goral

This Korean martial art involves lots of fast kicking

Taekwondo

Seoul

Golf is a popular sport in Korea. South Korea has produced several champion women players

Golf

Hån

Guinsa
This is the main temple of Korean Buddhism

Rose mallow
This is the national flower of South Korea

Ulsan

Nakdong

Busan

Daegu

Jinju

Sat at the top of Namsan mountain, this tower offers fantastic views of Seoul

Seoul Tower

Suwon

Incheon

Imjing

Haeju

Sejong City

Daejeon

SOUTH KOREA

Gwangju

Boseong Daehan Dawon tea plantation
This green-tea plantation in the mountain valleys of Boseong is a major tourist attraction

Annyeonghaseyo! Hello

YELLOW SEA

The island of Jeju is south of the Korean mainland

Jeju Island

Stone statues
Distinctive statues known as "dol hareubang", or stone grandfathers, are found on the island of Jeju.

N E W S

JAPAN

Japan is a modern, industrial country, but ancient traditions are still an important part of Japanese culture. Most people live in cities on one of the four main islands. Much of the country is mountainous with many active volcanoes.

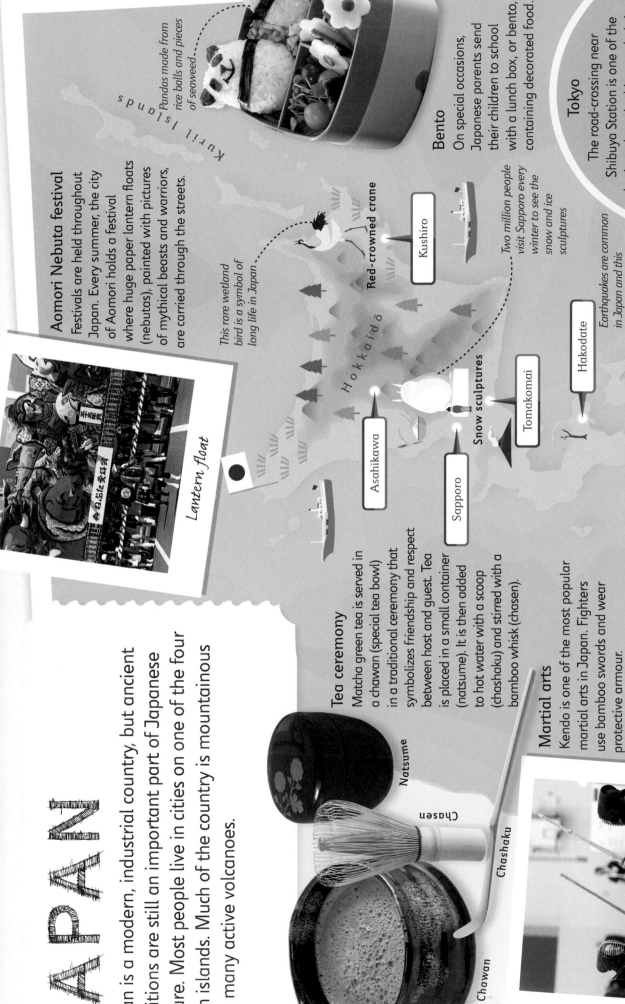

Kuril Islands

Hokkaidō

Honshū

JAPAN

RUSSIA

Kushiro
Asahikawa
Sapporo
Tomakomai
Hakodate
Aomori
Hirosaki
Sendai

Red-crowned crane

This rare wetland bird is a symbol of long life in Japan

Two million people visit Sapporo every winter to see the snow and ice sculptures

Snow sculptures

Earthquakes are common in Japan and this earthquake was the most powerful ever recorded in Japan

Tohoku earthquake

Aomori Nebuta festival
Festivals are held throughout Japan. Every summer, the city of Aomori holds a festival where huge paper lantern floats (nebutas), painted with pictures of mythical beasts and warriors, are carried through the streets.

Lantern float

Bento
On special occasions, Japanese parents send their children to school with a lunch box, or bento, containing decorated food.

Pandas made from rice balls and pieces of seaweed

Tokyo
The road-crossing near Shibuya Station is one of the busiest places in this crowded city. Often over 1,000 people, coming from all directions, will be on it at the same time.

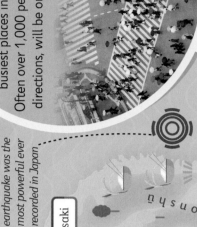

Tea ceremony
Matcha green tea is served in a chawan (special tea bowl) in a traditional ceremony that symbolizes friendship and respect between host and guest. Tea is placed in a small container (natsume). It is then added to hot water with a scoop (chashaku) and stirred with a bamboo whisk (chasen).

Natsume

Chasen

Chashaku

Chawan

Martial arts
Kendo is one of the most popular martial arts in Japan. Fighters use bamboo swords and wear protective armour.

Kendo

Comics and cartoons
Cartoon drawings are very popular in Japan. Comics in the distinctive hand-drawn style are called manga, while moving cartoons are known as anime.

Anime

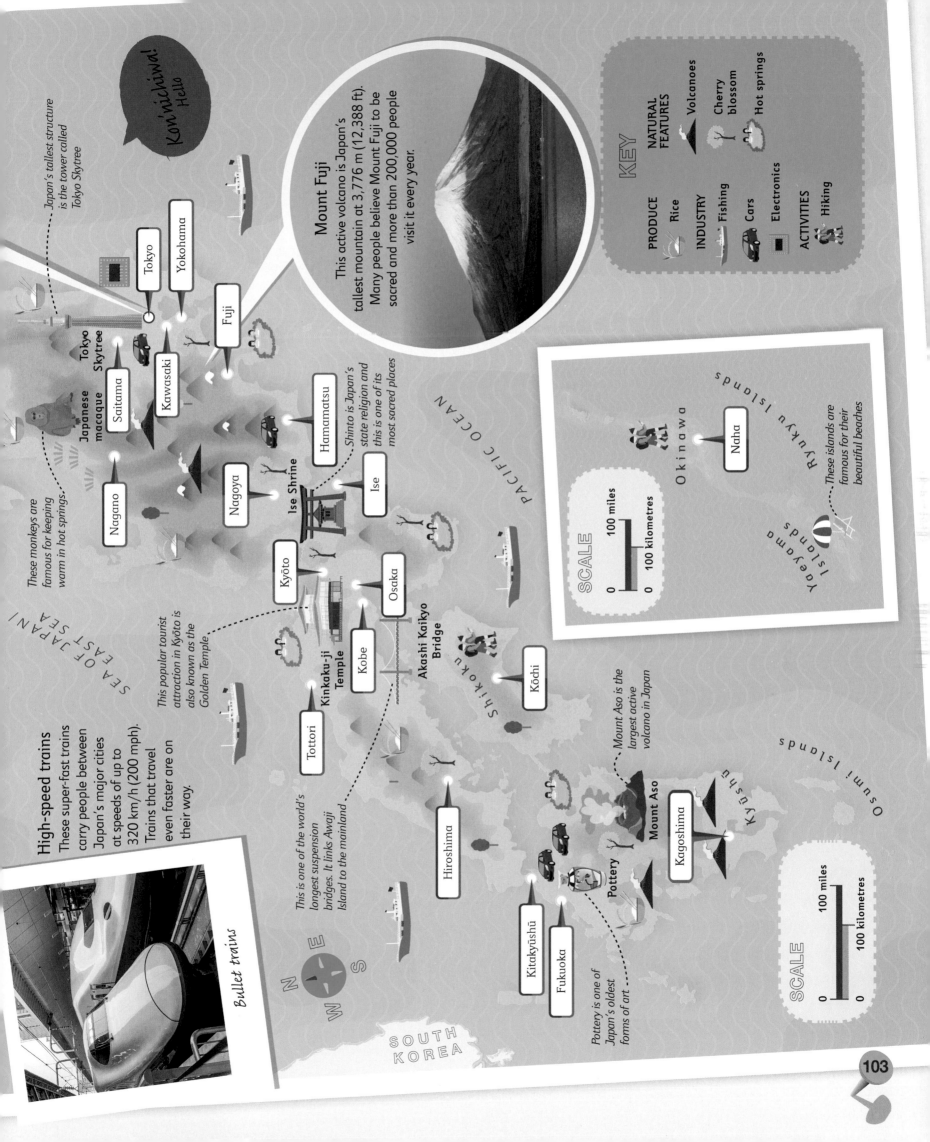

Kon'nichiwa!
Hello

Japan's tallest structure is the tower called Tokyo Skytree

Mount Fuji
This active volcano is Japan's tallest mountain at 3,776 m (12,388 ft). Many people believe Mount Fuji to be sacred and more than 200,000 people visit it every year.

KEY

NATURAL FEATURES
Volcanoes
Cherry blossom
Hot springs

PRODUCE
Rice

INDUSTRY
Fishing
Cars
Electronics

ACTIVITIES
Hiking

Tokyo
Yokohama
Fuji
Tokyo Skytree
Japanese macaque
Saitama
Kawasaki
Nagoya
Hamamatsu
Nagano
Ise Shrine
Ise

These monkeys are famous for keeping warm in hot springs.

Shinto is Japan's state religion and this is one of its most sacred places

Kyōto
Osaka
Kinkaku-ji Temple
Kobe
Akashi Kaikyo Bridge

This popular tourist attraction in Kyōto is also known as the Golden Temple

Tottori

Kōchi

PACIFIC OCEAN

SCALE
0   100 miles
0   100 kilometres

Naha

Okinawa
Ryukyu Islands

Yaeyama Islands

These islands are famous for their beautiful beaches

SEA OF JAPAN / EAST SEA

High-speed trains
These super-fast trains carry people between Japan's major cities at speeds of up to 320 km/h (200 mph). Trains that travel even faster are on their way.

This is one of the world's longest suspension bridges. It links Awaji Island to the mainland

Hiroshima

Shikoku

Mount Aso

Mount Aso is the largest active volcano in Japan

Kyūshū

Kagoshima

Osumi Islands

Pottery

Pottery is one of Japan's oldest forms of art

Kitakyūshū
Fukuoka

N
W   E
S

Bullet trains

SOUTH KOREA

SCALE
0   100 miles
0   100 kilometres

103

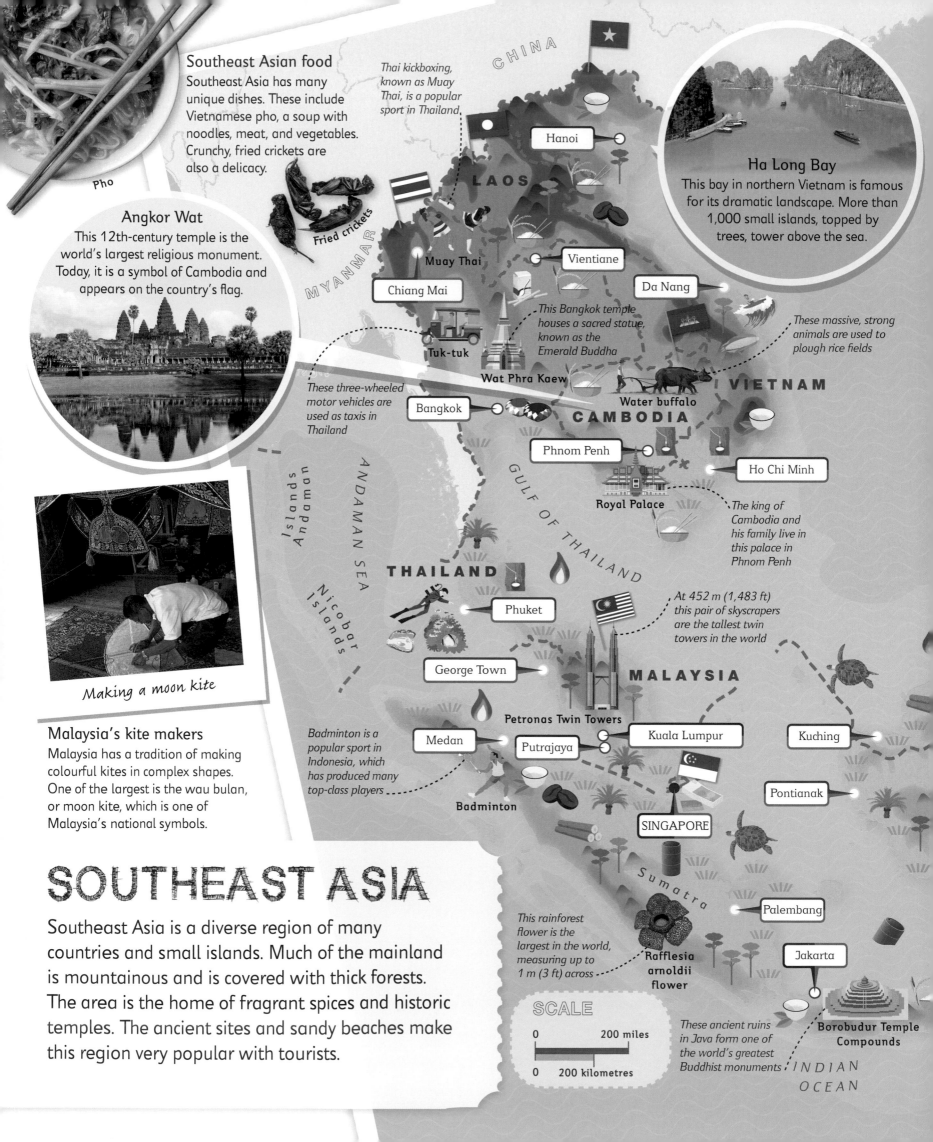

Southeast Asian food
Southeast Asia has many unique dishes. These include Vietnamese pho, a soup with noodles, meat, and vegetables. Crunchy, fried crickets are also a delicacy.

Pho

Fried crickets

Thai kickboxing, known as Muay Thai, is a popular sport in Thailand.

CHINA

Hanoi

LAOS

Ha Long Bay
This bay in northern Vietnam is famous for its dramatic landscape. More than 1,000 small islands, topped by trees, tower above the sea.

Angkor Wat
This 12th-century temple is the world's largest religious monument. Today, it is a symbol of Cambodia and appears on the country's flag.

MYANMAR

Muay Thai

Chiang Mai

Vientiane

Da Nang

This Bangkok temple houses a sacred statue, known as the Emerald Buddha

These massive, strong animals are used to plough rice fields

Tuk-tuk

Wat Phra Kaew

VIETNAM

Water buffalo

These three-wheeled motor vehicles are used as taxis in Thailand

Bangkok

CAMBODIA

Islands Andaman

ANDAMAN SEA

Phnom Penh

Ho Chi Minh

GULF OF THAILAND

Royal Palace

The king of Cambodia and his family live in this palace in Phnom Penh

Making a moon kite

THAILAND

Nicobar Islands

At 452 m (1,483 ft) this pair of skyscrapers are the tallest twin towers in the world

Phuket

Malaysia's kite makers
Malaysia has a tradition of making colourful kites in complex shapes. One of the largest is the wau bulan, or moon kite, which is one of Malaysia's national symbols.

George Town

MALAYSIA

Petronas Twin Towers

Badminton is a popular sport in Indonesia, which has produced many top-class players

Medan

Putrajaya

Kuala Lumpur

Kuching

Badminton

Pontianak

SINGAPORE

SOUTHEAST ASIA

Southeast Asia is a diverse region of many countries and small islands. Much of the mainland is mountainous and is covered with thick forests. The area is the home of fragrant spices and historic temples. The ancient sites and sandy beaches make this region very popular with tourists.

Sumatra

This rainforest flower is the largest in the world, measuring up to 1 m (3 ft) across

Palembang

Rafflesia arnoldii flower

Jakarta

SCALE

0 _____ 200 miles

0 _____ 200 kilometres

These ancient ruins in Java form one of the world's greatest Buddhist monuments

Borobudur Temple Compounds

INDIAN OCEAN

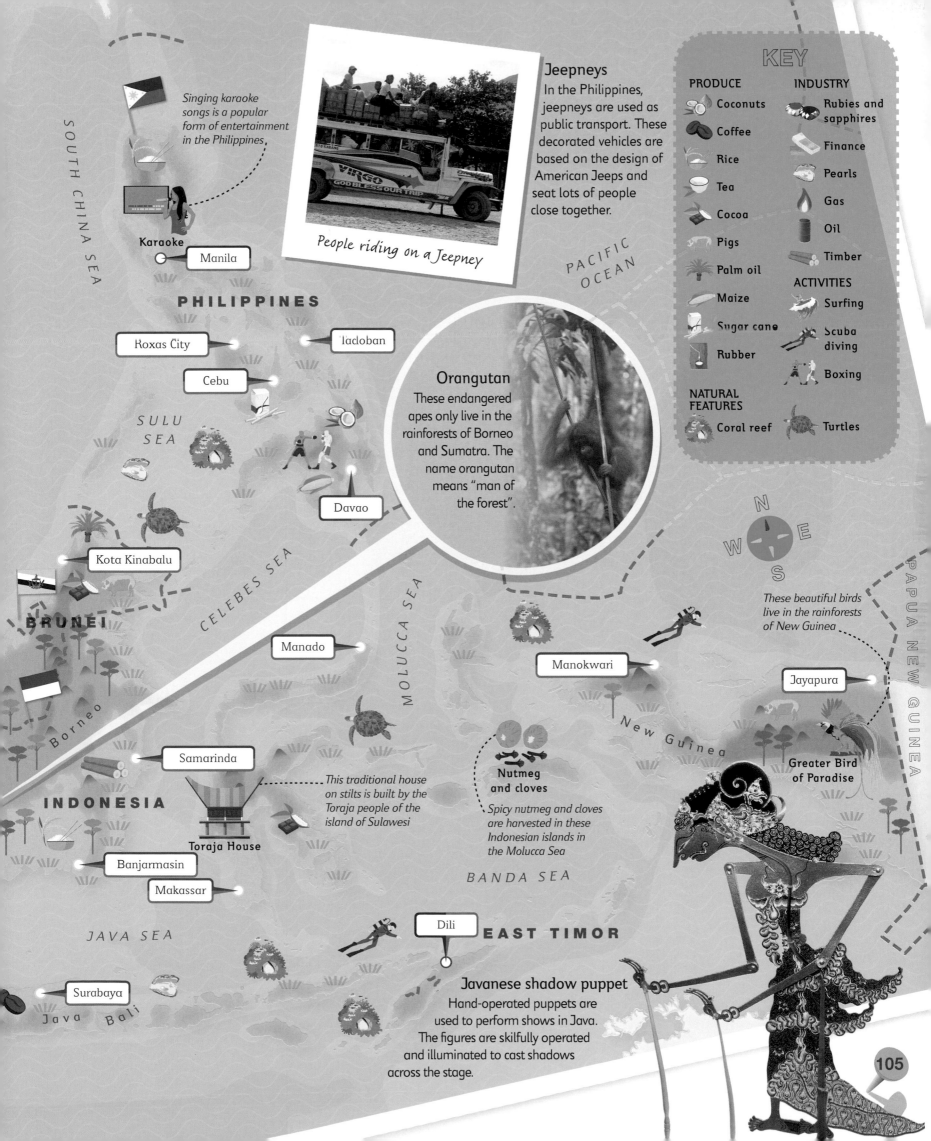

PRODUCE
- Coconuts
- Coffee
- Rice
- Tea
- Cocoa
- Pigs
- Palm oil
- Maize
- Sugar cane
- Rubber

INDUSTRY
- Rubies and sapphires
- Finance
- Pearls
- Gas
- Oil
- Timber

ACTIVITIES
- Surfing
- Scuba diving
- Boxing
- Turtles

NATURAL FEATURES
- Coral reef

Singing karaoke songs is a popular form of entertainment in the Philippines

Karaoke

Manila

Jeepneys
In the Philippines, jeepneys are used as public transport. These decorated vehicles are based on the design of American Jeeps and seat lots of people close together.

People riding on a Jeepney

SOUTH CHINA SEA

PACIFIC OCEAN

PHILIPPINES

Roxas City

Tacloban

Cebu

SULU SEA

Davao

Orangutan
These endangered apes only live in the rainforests of Borneo and Sumatra. The name orangutan means "man of the forest".

CELEBES SEA

MOLUCCA SEA

Kota Kinabalu

These beautiful birds live in the rainforests of New Guinea

BRUNEI

Manado

Manokwari

Jayapura

New Guinea

PAPUA NEW GUINEA

Borneo

Samarinda

This traditional house on stilts is built by the Toraja people of the island of Sulawesi

Nutmeg and cloves
Spicy nutmeg and cloves are harvested in these Indonesian islands in the Molucca Sea

Greater Bird of Paradise

INDONESIA

Toraja House

Banjarmasin

Makassar

BANDA SEA

JAVA SEA

Dili

EAST TIMOR

Surabaya

Java Bali

Javanese shadow puppet
Hand-operated puppets are used to perform shows in Java. The figures are skilfully operated and illuminated to cast shadows across the stage.

GREAT SITES

Throughout history, humans have built amazing structures and buildings. These great sites were often built to impress people and as a display of power. In the past, cathedrals and castles were among the largest and most awe-inspiring buildings. Today's spectacular buildings and structures include towering skyscrapers and long bridges.

OLDEST BUILDING

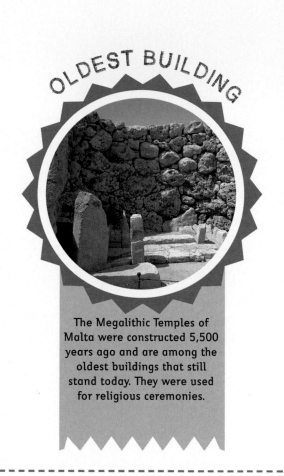

The Megalithic Temples of Malta were constructed 5,500 years ago and are among the oldest buildings that still stand today. They were used for religious ceremonies.

Six of the tallest buildings

Tall skyscrapers are built in cities, where land is expensive. Each of these buildings are the tallest in their respective continents. The Burj Khalifa is the tallest building in Asia and the world. It has 163 floors and contains apartments, restaurants, hotel rooms, and offices.

The Leonardo, Johannesburg, South Africa 234 m (768 ft) — Africa

Gran Torre Santiago, Santiago, Chile, 300 m (984 ft) — South America

Q1 Tower, Gold Coast, Australia 322.5 m (1,058 ft) — Australasia

Europe

Lakhta Center, St Petersburg, Russia 462 m (1,516 ft)

One World Trade Center, New York City, USA 541.3 m (1,776 ft) — North America

Burj Khalifa, Dubai, United Arab Emirates 828 m (2,717 ft) — Asia

Five of the longest bridges

Long bridges are built across rivers, lakes, harbours, valleys, and even swamps. Bridges are an important way of connecting communities.

Manchac Swamp Bridge, USA, 36.71 km (22.81 miles)

Lake Pontchartrain Causeway, USA, 38.35 km (23.83 miles)

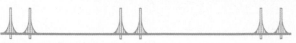

Bang Na Expressway, Thailand, 55 km (34.2 miles)

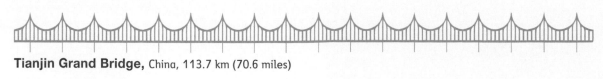

Tianjin Grand Bridge, China, 113.7 km (70.6 miles)

Danyang-Kunshan Grand Bridge, China, 164.8 km (102.4 miles)

The Danyang-Kunshan Grand Bridge carries a high-speed railway over rice paddies, rivers, and lakes.

Ten popular tourist attractions

These ten great sites are some of the most popular places for tourists to visit. They include historic buildings, religious sites, and ancient monuments.

Golden Gate Bridge, San Francisco, USA

Forbidden City, Beijing, China

Angkor Wat, Siem Reap, Cambodia

Eiffel Tower, Paris, France

Great Pyramid of Giza, Giza, Egypt

La Sagrada Família, Barcelona, Spain

Hagia Sophia, Istanbul, Turkey

Uluru, Northern Territory, Australia

Machu Picchu, Andes, Peru

St Peter's Basilica, Vatican City

New Seven Wonders of the World

In 2007, a worldwide survey voted the great sites shown here as being the New Seven Wonders of the World. The original Seven Wonders of the Ancient World included the Great Pyramid at Giza, Egypt.

1. CHICHEN ITZA, Mexico

This ancient city was built by the Mayans. It has many great stone buildings, including this pyramid, called El Castillo.

2. MACHU PICCHU, Peru

Nestled in the Andes, this stone city built by the Incas is now in ruins. The name Machu Picchu means "old mountain".

4. COLOSSEUM, Italy

The Romans built this massive, oval-shaped stadium. It could seat more than 50,000 people. Gladiators fought in it.

6. TAJ MAHAL, India

The Taj Mahal means "crown of palaces". It was built as a tomb for Mumtaz Mahal, wife of the Mughal emperor Shah Jahan.

3. CHRIST THE REDEEMER, Brazil

This huge statue of Jesus Christ is 30 m (98 ft) tall. It is carved out of soapstone and looms over Rio de Janeiro in Brazil.

5. PETRA, Jordan

The ancient city of Petra was carved out of rocky cliffs. It is also known as the "Rose City", because of the rock's pink colour.

7. GREAT WALL OF CHINA, China

The longest man-made structure, the Great Wall is an amazing sight as it winds its way through the mountains of China.

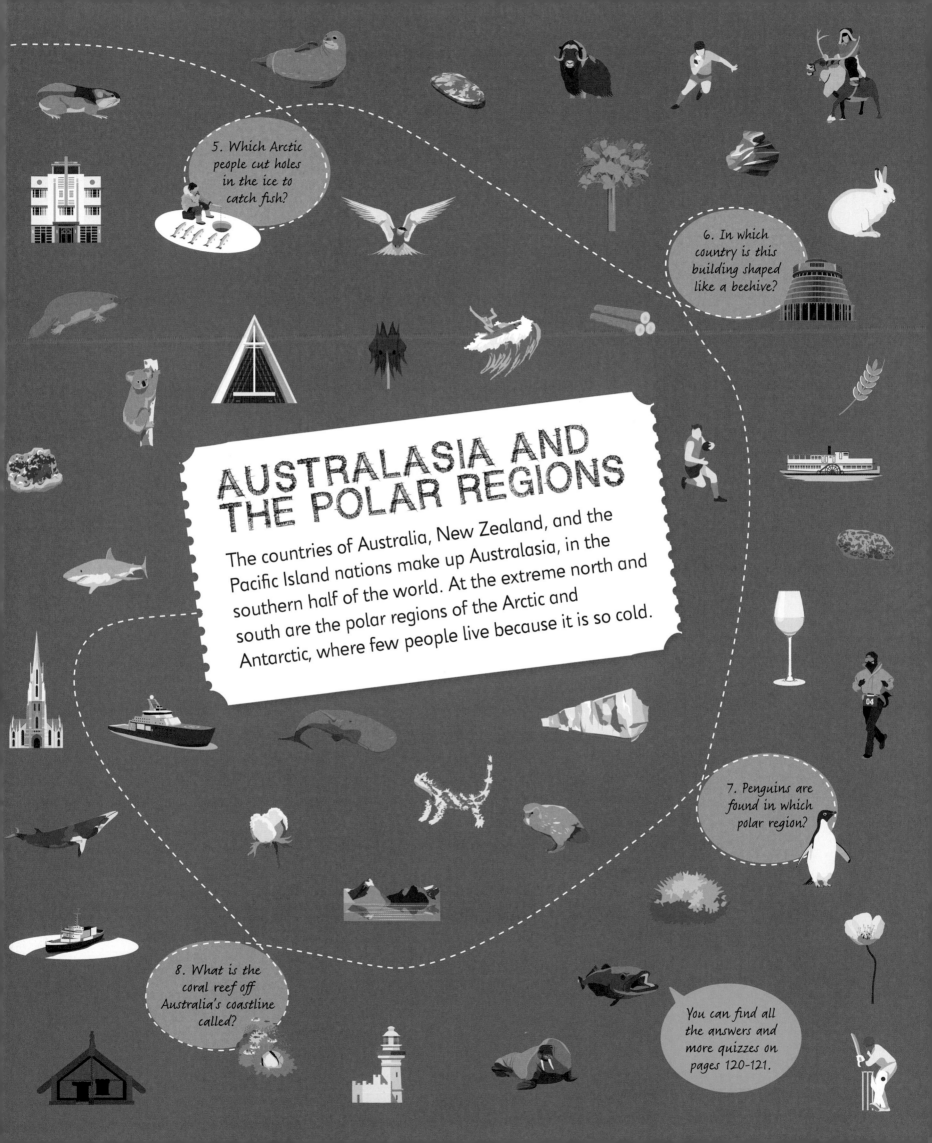

AUSTRALASIA AND THE POLAR REGIONS

The countries of Australia, New Zealand, and the Pacific Island nations make up Australasia, in the southern half of the world. At the extreme north and south are the polar regions of the Arctic and Antarctic, where few people live because it is so cold

5. Which Arctic people cut holes in the ice to catch fish?

6. In which country is this building shaped like a beehive?

7. Penguins are found in which polar region?

8. What is the coral reef off Australia's coastline called?

You can find all the answers and more quizzes on pages 120-121.

AUSTRALASIA

The vast region of Australasia contains a wide variety of different landscapes, ranging from the desert that covers most of Australia to tropical islands dotted around the Pacific Ocean, which are fringed with golden, sandy beaches and coral reefs. There are also large areas of dense rainforest in eastern Australia, Tasmania, Papua New Guinea, and New Zealand.

The dotted lines show where these island groups are, as many are too small to show up on this map

PHILIPPINE SEA

Northern Mariana Islands **(UNITED STATES)**

Guam **(UNITED STATES)**

PALAU

MICRONESIA

PAPUA NEW GUINEA

ARAFURA SEA

TIMOR SEA

Christmas Island **(AUSTRALIA)**

Cocos (Keeling) Islands **(AUSTRALIA)**

Ashmore and Cartier Islands **(AUSTRALIA)**

Coral Sea Islands **(AUSTRALIA)**

CORAL SEA

INDIAN OCEAN

Northern Territory

Western Australia

AUSTRALIA

Queensland

South Australia

New South Wales

Victoria

Tasmania

Perth

This coastal city is the capital of the state of Western Australia. Its centre is crammed with modern, high-rise buildings. Although it is one of the world's most isolated cities, Perth is home to people from many different countries and cultures.

Uluru

This unique, sandstone rock formation rises up majestically from the desert of Australia's Northern Territory and is of great spiritual and cultural importance to Australia's Aboriginal people.

SCALE

0	500 miles	1000 miles

0	1000 kilometres

French Polynesia
A group of 118 far-flung Pacific islands makes up this territory that belongs to France, although it is a long way from Europe. The islands have beautiful beaches and coral reefs.

Wake Island
(UNITED STATES)

MARSHALL ISLANDS

NAURU

Kingman Reef
(UNITED STATES)

Palmyra Atoll
(UNITED STATES)

Baker and Howland Islands
(UNITED STATES)

Jarvis Island
(UNITED STATES)

K I R I B A T I

TUVALU

Tokelau
(NEW ZEALAND)

SOLOMON ISLANDS

Wallis and Futuna
(FRANCE)

SAMOA

American Samoa
(UNITED STATES)

VANUATU

Cook Islands
(NEW ZEALAND)

Niue
(NEW ZEALAND)

French Polynesia
(FRANCE)

FIJI

TONGA

New Caledonia
(FRANCE)

Pitcairn, Henderson, Ducie, and Oeno Islands
(UNITED KINGDOM)

Norfolk Island
(AUSTRALIA)

rd Howe Island
(AUSTRALIA)

Kermadec Islands
(NEW ZEALAND)

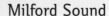
PACIFIC OCEAN

NEW ZEALAND

A S M A N S E A

Chatham Islands
(NEW ZEALAND)

Bounty Islands
(NEW ZEALAND)

Auckland Islands
(NEW ZEALAND)

Antipodes Islands
(NEW ZEALAND)

Campbell Islands
(NEW ZEALAND)

Macquarie Island
(AUSTRALIA)

Coral reefs
Some of the world's most colourful corals and tropical fish live in the warm waters of the Pacific Ocean. The most amazing coral reef is the Great Barrier Reef off the northeast coast of Australia.

Milford Sound

The waters of this beautiful fjord, on the southwest coast of New Zealand's South Island, flow almost 15 km (9 miles) inland from the Tasman Sea. Majestic cliffs sweep up 1,200 m (3,900 ft) on either side. Every year, nearly a million people visit this stunning site.

AUSTRALIA

Australia is a huge island between the Indian and Pacific Oceans. The middle of Australia is a vast desert known as the "Outback", which is extremely hot and dry. Most Australians live around the coastal areas, where it is cooler. Here, many people enjoy outdoor activities, such as surfing.

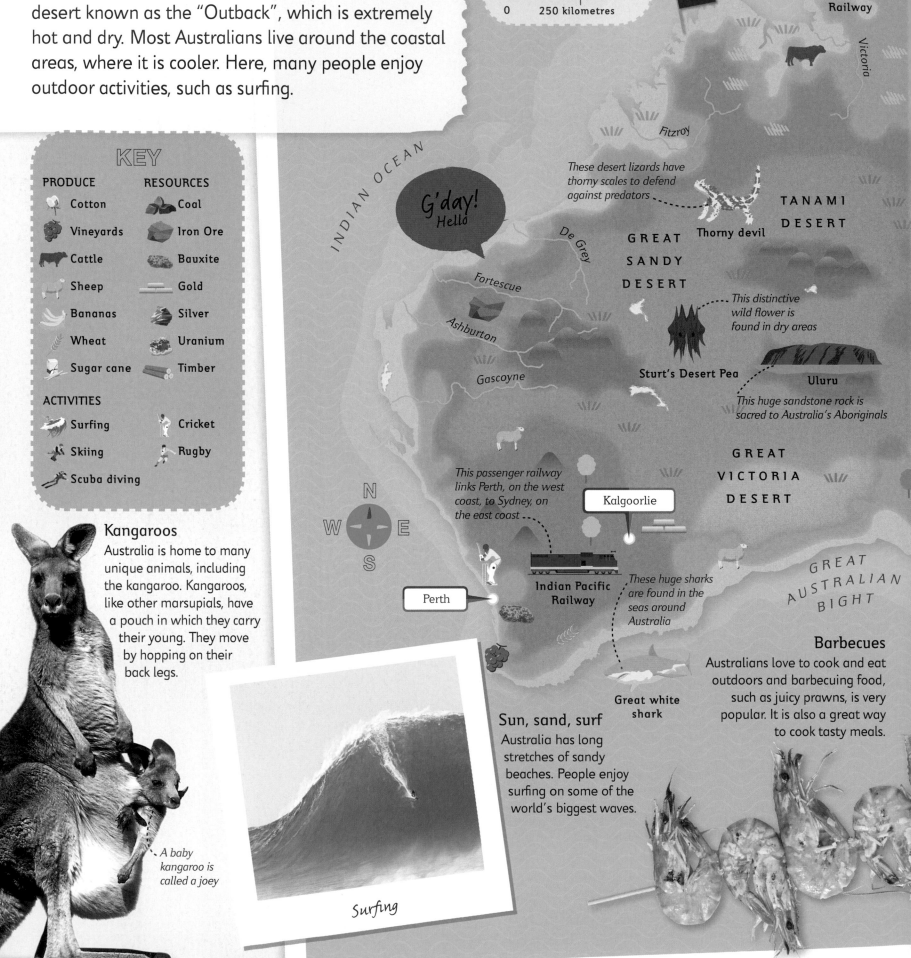

SCALE

0   250 miles

0   250 kilometres

KEY

PRODUCE
- Cotton
- Vineyards
- Cattle
- Sheep
- Bananas
- Wheat
- Sugar cane

RESOURCES
- Coal
- Iron Ore
- Bauxite
- Gold
- Silver
- Uranium
- Timber

ACTIVITIES
- Surfing
- Skiing
- Scuba diving
- Cricket
- Rugby

TIMOR SEA

Darwin

This railway runs from Darwin to Adelaide, a journey of 2,979 km (1,851 miles)

The Ghan Railway

Victoria

Fitzroy

INDIAN OCEAN

G'day! Hello

De Grey

Fortescue

Ashburton

Gascoyne

These desert lizards have thorny scales to defend against predators

Thorny devil

TANAMI DESERT

GREAT SANDY DESERT

This distinctive wild flower is found in dry areas

Sturt's Desert Pea

Uluru

This huge sandstone rock is sacred to Australia's Aboriginals

GREAT VICTORIA DESERT

This passenger railway links Perth, on the west coast, to Sydney, on the east coast

Kalgoorlie

N W E S

Perth

Indian Pacific Railway

These huge sharks are found in the seas around Australia

Great white shark

GREAT AUSTRALIAN BIGHT

Kangaroos

Australia is home to many unique animals, including the kangaroo. Kangaroos, like other marsupials, have a pouch in which they carry their young. They move by hopping on their back legs.

A baby kangaroo is called a joey

Sun, sand, surf

Australia has long stretches of sandy beaches. People enjoy surfing on some of the world's biggest waves.

Barbecues

Australians love to cook and eat outdoors and barbecuing food, such as juicy prawns, is very popular. It is also a great way to cook tasty meals.

Surfing

ARAFURA SEA

Aboriginal paintings of European ships arriving in the 18th century feature on rocks in this park

Kakadu National Park

This egg-laying mammal is only found in Australia

GULF OF CARPENTARIA

PAPUA NEW GUINEA

PACIFIC OCEAN

CORAL SEA

All kinds of colourful fish make their home among the corals of the Great Barrier Reef

Mitchell

Duck-billed Platypus

GREAT BARRIER REEF

Cairns

Flinders

AUSTRALIA

Townsville

To reach remote areas, doctors have to travel in light aircraft

Alice Springs

Flying Doctors

These bear-like animals live in and eat the leaves of eucalyptus, or gum trees

SIMPSON DESERT

Australia's national gemstone is found in many bright colours, including green, blue, and yellow

Macadamia trees are native to Australia and their nuts are a tasty food crop

Koala

This bright lighthouse on Australia's easternmost point helps keep ships safe

Brisbane

Opal

These traditional paddle steamer boats still travel on the Darling and Murray rivers

Macadamia nuts

Darling

Cape Byron Lighthouse

These lakes dry up and disappear in hot, dry months

This formation of three towering rocks is in the Blue Mountains

Three Sisters Rocks

Paddle Steamer

Adelaide

Murray

Sydney

Canberra

This sport has two teams of 18 players and is only played professionally in Australia

Australian football

Melbourne

This major horse race is one of the biggest sporting events in Australia

Melbourne Cup

TASMAN SEA

This waterfall is in the Tasmanian Wilderness area

Tasmania

Nelson Falls

Hobart

Great Barrier Reef
The world's largest coral reefs are off the northeastern coast of Australia. They cover about the same area as Japan and are a great site for scuba divers.

Aboriginals
The Aboriginals were the first people to live in Australia. Some have held onto their traditions and are skilled at finding food in the bush, such as witchetty grubs (larvae of moths).

Digging for food

Opera House
Sydney is Australia's oldest and largest city. Its opera house stands in the city's harbour. It is instantly recognizable because of its dramatic shape. The roofs look like the sails of a ship.

Tasmanian devil
These fierce animals are the size of a small dog and only live in the wild in Tasmania. They are named "devils" because of their aggressive character.

113

All Blacks rugby team

The All Blacks is the nickname of the national men's rugby union team. It is one of the best rugby teams in the world. The men perform a *haka*, a traditional Māori war dance, before each international match.

The haka

PACIFIC OCEAN

Kiwi

This flightless bird is native to New Zealand. It is the country's national symbol and appears on coins and badges. New Zealanders are often referred to as "Kiwis".

The Māori people built wooden meeting houses, often with detailed carving on the outside

Carved meeting house

Whangarei

Kauri

This huge tree only grows on New Zealand's North Island. It can be up to 50 m (164 ft) tall with a 5 m (16 ft) diameter trunk

Auckland

Hamilton

BAY OF PLENTY

Rotorua

Gisborne

Waikato

Lake Taupo

Hawke Bay

Napier

Napier has many Art Deco buildings, which were built after an earthquake in the 1930s

Art Deco building

North Island

New Plymouth

Mt Taranaki

This active volcano last erupted in the mid-19th century

Palmerston North

Māori club

Māori warriors used short-handled clubs to strike their enemies in battle. They were made from whale bone, hard volcanic rock, wood, and sometimes iron. Some were elaborately carved.

The Prime Minister and his cabinet work in this building. It is known as "the beehive" because of its shape

"Beehive" Parliament building

Wellington

Nelson

Blenheim

TASMAN SEA

Pohutu Geyser

"Pohutu" means explosion or big splash. Hot water from this geyser spurts up into the air about 20 times a day, reaching heights of around 30 m (100 ft).

SCALE

0   50 miles
0   50 kilometres

KEY

PRODUCE
- Sheep
- Cattle
- Vineyards
- Apples and pears
- Peaches
- Wheat

INDUSTRY
- Hydroelectric power
- Oil
- Gas
- Coal
- Gold

ACTIVITIES
- Skiing
- Hiking
- Fishing
- Mountain biking
- White-water rafting
- Sailing
- Hot springs

NATURAL FEATURES
- Earthquakes
- Volcanoes

N E S W

NEW ZEALAND

New Zealand is one of the world's most isolated countries, being nearly 1,500 km (930 miles) from its nearest neighbour, Australia. It is made up of two large islands and several smaller ones. Farmland and forests cover much of the country. Volcanic activity has created many high mountains and hot springs.

Cardboard Cathedral

An earthquake severely damaged Christchurch's cathedral in 2011. A cardboard, steel, and timber replacement was built nearby to use while repairs are carried out.

Māori

Māoris were the first people to arrive in New Zealand, nearly 1,000 years ago. Today, they make up less than a quarter of the population, but interest in their culture is growing. Children can now learn the Māori language at school.

Māori dancers

Large numbers of sperm whales feed in the waters near Kaikoura

Sperm whale

Kaikoura

Christchurch

Sauvignon Blanc

p u a l s I y y n o S
South Island

Hello!

Greymouth

SOUTHERN ALPS

New Zealand's climate is ideal for growing grapes for making wine, and the country is famous for its high-quality Sauvignon Blanc wine

Waitaki

This impressive church seats more than 1,000 people - **First Church**

Dunedin

Clutha

Invercargill

This very rare parrot cannot fly. It is also called the owl parrot, because it only comes out at night

Kakapo

Stewart Island

FIORDLAND

Milford Sound

Despite its remote location, this beautiful fjord is one of New Zealand's most visited sites

PACIFIC OCEAN

Glaciers

New Zealand has many glaciers, mostly on South Island. One of the largest is the Franz Josef glacier, named after an Austrian emperor by a German explorer. This massive block of ice is 12 km (7½ miles) long.

Hiking on Franz Josef glacier

Farming and fishing

New Zealand exports its produce all over the world. It is famous for its lamb and juicy, green-fleshed kiwi fruit. Large, green-lipped mussels live around the coast and are also farmed.

Green-lipped mussels

Kiwi fruit

ANTARCTICA

Antarctica is the coldest and driest continent on Earth. More than 99 per cent of the land is covered by a huge ice sheet, which is up to 4.5 km (2¾ miles) thick in places. No people live there permanently, but scientists and tourists visit to study this icy world and its unique animals and plants.

Krill

The cold waters of the Southern Ocean are full of krill. These little shrimp-like animals are the main source of food for many birds and whales.

Antarctic stations

Scientists live and work in Antarctica in research stations. *Halley VI* is a British station that has eight units, which can be moved independently. Each unit sits above the ice on stilts with skis.

Halley VI dining unit

Larsen B Ice Shelf

This huge area of ice on the edge of the Weddell Sea melted and broke up in 2002 as a result of global climate change.

Emperor penguins

Penguins cannot fly. Instead, they use their wings to swim underwater to search for krill and fish. Emperor penguins breed on the ice during the winter, with each pair raising one chick.

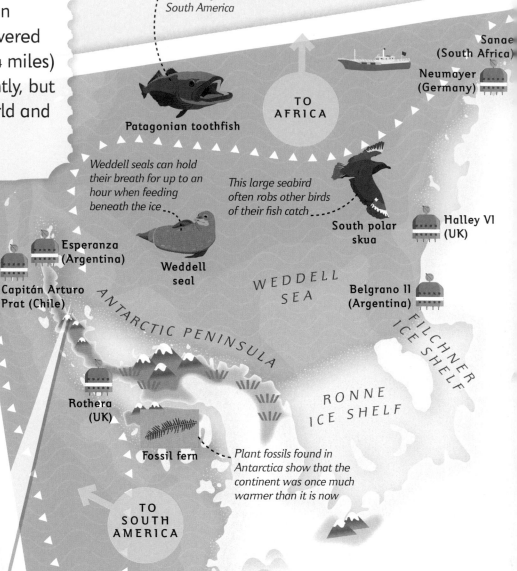

This species of cod icefish is fished by trawlers from South America

TO AFRICA

Sanae (South Africa)

Neumayer (Germany)

Patagonian toothfish

Weddell seals can hold their breath for up to an hour when feeding beneath the ice

This large seabird often robs other birds of their fish catch

South polar skua

Halley VI (UK)

Esperanza (Argentina)

Weddell seal

WEDDELL SEA

Belgrano II (Argentina)

Capitán Arturo Prat (Chile)

ANTARCTIC PENINSULA

FILCHNER ICE SHELF

Rothera (UK)

RONNE ICE SHELF

Fossil fern

Plant fossils found in Antarctica show that the continent was once much warmer than it is now

TO SOUTH AMERICA

West Antarctica

SOUTHERN OCEAN

Limit of summer pack ice

Limit of winter pack ice

Icebergs are huge, floating chunks of ice that have broken off ice shelves and glaciers

Iceberg

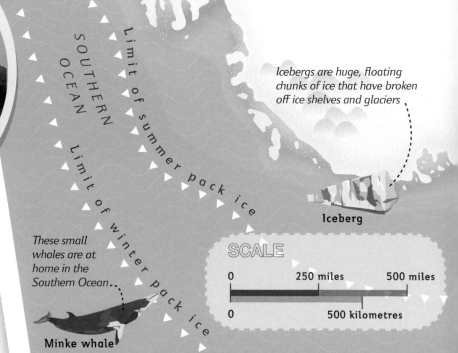

SCALE

0	250 miles	500 miles

0	500 kilometres

These small whales are at home in the Southern Ocean

Minke whale

Maitri
(India)

SOUTHERN
OCEAN

Syowa
(Japan)

These ships can break through ice up to 1 m (3 ft) thick ..... **Research ship**

Zhongshan
(China)

Taishan
(China)

Davis
(Australia)

East Antarctica

Roald Amundsen

Meteorites
Rocks from space that land on the Earth's surface are called meteorites. Thousands of meteorites have been collected from Antarctica, including ones from the Moon and the planet Mars.

Scientists examining a meteorite

Amundsen-Scott
(USA)

South
Pole

Vostok
(Russia)

South
Geomagnetic
Pole

TRANSANTARCTIC MOUNTAINS

ROSS ICE
SHELF

Rugby

Every summer, Scott station rugby club plays a game on the snow against a team from McMurdo station

Scott (NZ)

McMurdo (USA)

The Ice Marathon has been held every summer since 2006, and even the penguins have been known to join in!

ROSS SEA

Mario Zucchelli
(Italy)

Ice Marathon

This powerful seal eats krill, penguins, and other seals

More than 2 million pairs of Adélie penguins breed around Antarctica every year, nesting on ice-free areas of rock

Dumont
d'Urville
(France)

TO
AUSTRALIA

TO
NEW
ZEALAND

Leopard seal

Adélie penguin

Race to the South Pole
Explorers competed to be the first people to reach the South Pole, the southernmost point on Earth. The Norwegian Roald Amundsen led the first successful team there in 1911.

KEY

**NATURAL
FEATURES**

Volcanoes

ACTIVITIES

Cross-
country
skiing

OTHER

Research
stations

Fishing
trawler

117

THE ARCTIC

The extreme northern edges of the countries of the USA, Europe, Asia, and North America lie within the Arctic region. At its centre lies the North Pole. Most of the Arctic is ice, floating above the Arctic Ocean. In summer, the ice shrinks and chunks break off into the ocean. In winter, the ice expands.

Inuit carving

The Inuit are a group of people that live in the Arctic regions of the USA, Canada, and Greenland. They have created carvings of animal figures, made from walrus tusks.

Polar bear

The polar bear's thick fur helps it keep warm in freezing Arctic temperatures. It hunts mainly seals, which it catches through holes in the ice. It is also a very good swimmer.

KEY

INDUSTRY
- Oil
- Gold
- Gas
- Copper
- Iron

PRODUCE
- Salmon

ACTIVITIES
- Cross-country skiing

Lemmings live on the tundra, a treeless area around the Arctic.

Brown lemming

Khatanga

Arctic willow

This tiny willow is the northernmost woody plant in the world.

Tiksi

LAPTEV SEA

RUSSIA

The Chukchi people of the Russian Arctic depend on their reindeer herds for food and transport

Arctic tern

These birds breed in the Arctic when it is summer there, then fly to Antarctica to enjoy the southern summer

Pevek

Chukchi

EAST SIBERIAN SEA

ARCTIC OCEAN

CHUKCHI SEA

Walruses hunt for food in the sea and rest on land or floating ice

The Arctic Circle is an imaginary circle that marks the edge of the Arctic region

Walrus

Barrow

BEAUFORT SEA

Musk oxen use their large, curved horns to defend themselves against polar bears and wolves

Prudhoe Bay

USA

Inuvik

Musk ox

SCALE

0   250 miles

0   250 kilometres

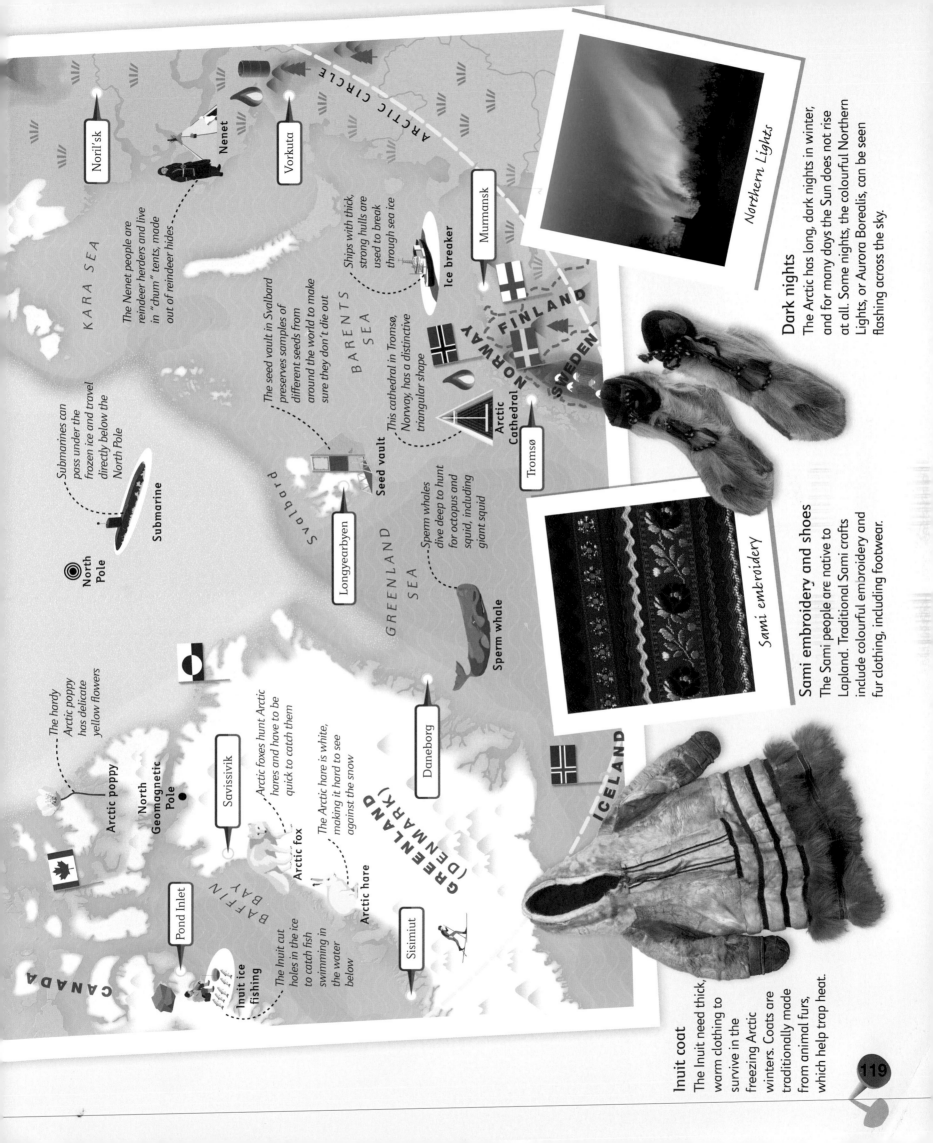

ARCTIC CIRCLE

Noril'sk

Nenet

The Nenet people are reindeer herders and live in "chum" tents, made out of reindeer hides

Vorkuta

KARA SEA

Submarines can pass under the frozen ice and travel directly below the North Pole

Submarine

◎ North Pole

The seed vault in Svalbard preserves samples of different seeds from around the world to make sure they don't die out

BARENTS SEA

Ships with thick, strong hulls are used to break through sea ice

Ice breaker

Murmansk

FINLAND

NORWAY

SWEDEN

This cathedral in Tromsø, Norway, has a distinctive triangular shape

Arctic Cathedral

Tromsø

Svalbard

Longyearbyen

Seed vault

GREENLAND SEA

Sperm whales dive deep to hunt for octopus and squid, including giant squid

Sperm whale

Northern Lights

Dark nights
The Arctic has long, dark nights in winter, and for many days the Sun does not rise at all. Some nights, the colourful Northern Lights, or Aurora Borealis, can be seen flashing across the sky.

Sami embroidery

Sami embroidery and shoes
The Sami people are native to Lapland. Traditional Sami crafts include colourful embroidery and fur clothing, including footwear.

The hardy Arctic poppy has delicate yellow flowers

Arctic poppy

North Geomagnetic Pole

Savissivik

Arctic foxes hunt Arctic hares and have to be quick to catch them

Arctic fox

The Arctic hare is white, making it hard to see against the snow

Arctic hare

GREENLAND (DENMARK)

Daneborg

ICELAND

Pond Inlet

BAFFIN BAY

The Inuit cut holes in the ice to catch fish swimming in the water below

Inuit ice fishing

CANADA

Sisimiut

Inuit coat
The Inuit need thick, warm clothing to survive in the freezing Arctic winters. Coats are traditionally made from animal furs, which help trap heat.

ATLAS PICTURE QUIZ

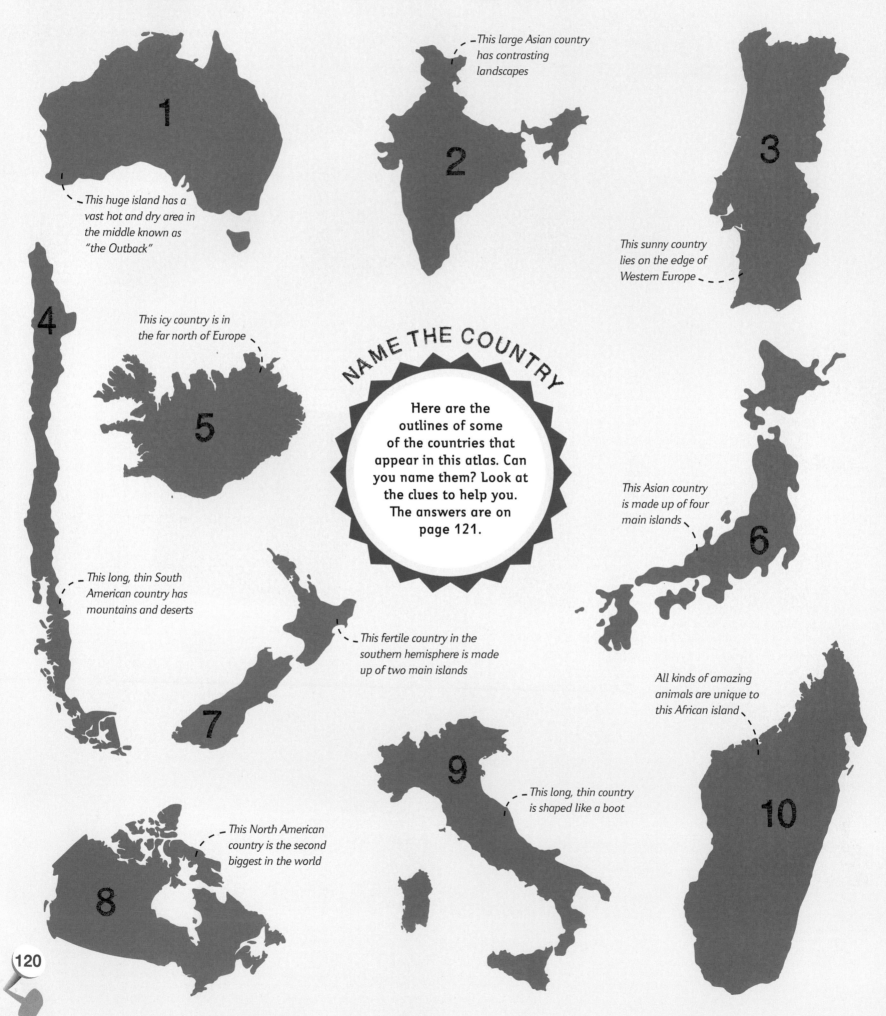

This large Asian country has contrasting landscapes

1

This huge island has a vast hot and dry area in the middle known as "the Outback"

2

3

This sunny country lies on the edge of Western Europe

4

This icy country is in the far north of Europe

5

NAME THE COUNTRY

Here are the outlines of some of the countries that appear in this atlas. Can you name them? Look at the clues to help you. The answers are on page 121.

This Asian country is made up of four main islands

6

This long, thin South American country has mountains and deserts

This fertile country in the southern hemisphere is made up of two main islands

7

All kinds of amazing animals are unique to this African island

9

This long, thin country is shaped like a boot

10

This North American country is the second biggest in the world

8

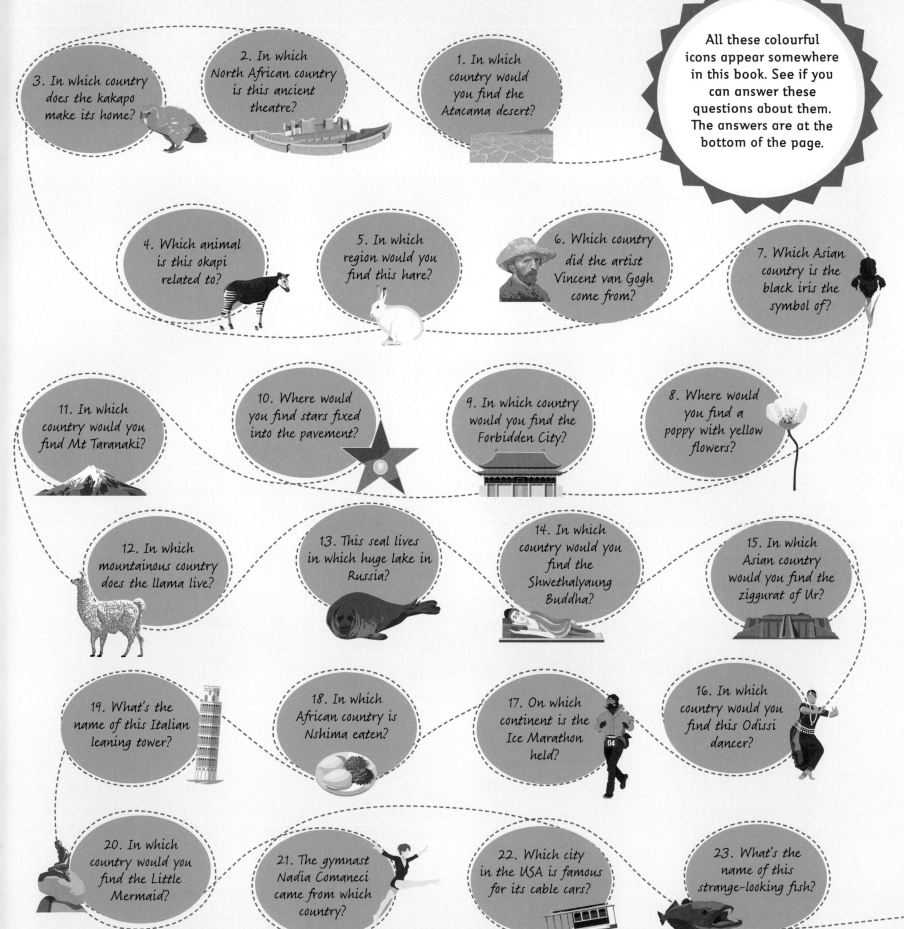

All these colourful icons appear somewhere in this book. See if you can answer these questions about them. The answers are at the bottom of the page.

3. In which country does the kakapo make its home?

2. In which North African country is this ancient theatre?

1. In which country would you find the Atacama desert?

4. Which animal is this okapi related to?

5. In which region would you find this hare?

6. Which country did the artist Vincent van Gogh come from?

7. Which Asian country is the black iris the symbol of?

11. In which country would you find Mt Taranaki?

10. Where would you find stars fixed into the pavement?

9. In which country would you find the Forbidden City?

8. Where would you find a poppy with yellow flowers?

12. In which mountainous country does the llama live?

13. This seal lives in which huge lake in Russia?

14. In which country would you find the Shwethalyaung Buddha?

15. In which Asian country would you find the ziggurat of Ur?

19. What's the name of this Italian leaning tower?

18. In which African country is Nshima eaten?

17. On which continent is the Ice Marathon held?

16. In which country would you find this Odissi dancer?

20. In which country would you find the Little Mermaid?

21. The gymnast Nadia Comaneci came from which country?

22. Which city in the USA is famous for its cable cars?

23. What's the name of this strange-looking fish?

Answers: Page 8 – 9 North America: 1.Mount Rushmore, 2.Dominican Republic, 3.Toronto, 4.Mexico, 5.New York, 6.Colorado River, 7.Inuit, 8.Panama Canal. **Page 22 – 23 South America:** 1.Rio de Janeiro, 2.Andes, 3. Colombia, 4.Chile, 5.Brazil, 6.Argentina, 7.Spectacled bear, 8.Peru. **Page 34 – 35 Africa:** 1.Tuareg, 2.Kenya, 3.Libya, 4.Felucca, 5.Congo, 6.South Africa, 7.Zambia, 8.Madagascar. **Page 50 – 51 Europe:** 1.Corsica, 2.St. Basil's cathedral, 3.England, 4.Salzburg, 5.Czech Republic, 6.France, 7.River Danube, 8.Spain. **Page 80 – 81 Asia:** 1.India, 2.Turkey, 3.Turkey, 4.Mongolia, 5.Taiwan, 6.China, 7.Tokyo Skytree, 8.South Korea. **Page 108 – 109 Australasia and the Polar Regions:** 1.Arctic fox, 2.Tasmania, 3.Australia, 4.Uluru, 5.Inuit, 6. New Zealand, 7.Antarctica, 8.Great Barrier Reef. **Page 120 Name the Country:** 1.Australia, 2.India, 3.Portugal, 4.Chile, 5.Iceland, 6.Japan, 7.New Zealand, 8.Canada, 9.Italy, 10.Madagascar. **Page 121 Guess the Icon:** 1.Chile, 2.Algeria, 3.New Zealand, 4.Giraffe, 5.Arctic, 6.Netherlands, 7.Jordan, 8.Arctic, 9. China, 10.Los Angeles, 11.New Zealand, 12.Peru, 13.Lake Baikal, 14.Myanmar, 15.Iraq, 16.India, 17.Antarctica, 18.Zambia, 19.Tower of Pisa, 20.Denmark, 21.Romania, 22.San Francisco, 23.Patagonian toothfish.

GLOSSARY

aboriginals
Original or first-known inhabitants of a country. It is mainly used to refer to the native people of Australia

artefact
Man-made object, generally of historic or cultural interest, such as a painting or a vase

canyon
Deep, narrow valley with very steep, rocky sides. A stream or river usually flows through it

capital
Country's most important city. It is where the government usually meets and passes laws

climate
Normal weather pattern during the year in any part of the world

continents
Seven large areas of land that the world is divided into: Africa, Antarctica, Asia, Australasia, Europe, North America, and South America

coral reef
Rock-like structure formed by a group of corals (simple sea animals) in the warm waters along tropical coasts. Many fish and other sea creatures live around coral reefs

country
Area of Earth that is governed by the same leaders and has the same flag. Most continents are made up of many different countries

crops
Plants grown to feed people and animals. Crops need the right soil and climate to grow well

culture
Way of life and beliefs of the people of a region or country

delta
Flat land formed from material deposited by a river around the area where it enters the sea or flows into a lake. Soil in a delta area is usually very fertile

desert
Dry region that gets 25 cm (10 in) or less of rainfall in a year. Deserts can be hot or cold. Only a few animals and plants are able to live in desert areas

dunes
Mounds or ridges of sand that are formed by the wind or flowing water pushing the sand together. They are usually found along beaches or in sandy deserts.

earthquake
Movement of large blocks of rock beneath the Earth's surface. Cracks may open up in the ground, causing buildings to collapse

endangered
Word used to describe a species of plant or animal with only a few living members left

Equator
Imaginary line around the Earth, which is exactly halfway between the North and South Poles. Countries close to the Equator are hotter than countries that are further away from it

ethnic group
Group of people who share the same racial, religious, or cultural background

exports
Goods or services that are sold to another country

extinct
Word used to describe a plant or animal species that has no living members. All dinosaurs, for example, are now extinct

fertile land
Land where the soil is particularly good for growing crops on

fjord
Long, narrow bay or inlet, with steep, high, rocky sides. The word is Norwegian and was first used to describe the many deep inlets along Norway's rocky coast

fossil
Remains or shape of a prehistoric plant or animal that have been preserved in rock

game reserve
Area where wild animals are protected from hunters, or where hunting is limited by law. Africa has many game reserves

geyser
Fountain of hot water and steam that shoots up out of the ground. Geysers form when an underground stream flows over hot, volcanic rocks

glacier
Huge, thick sheet of ice moving very slowly, either down the side of a mountain or over an area of land. Glaciers help to shape and form the landscape

grasslands
Open land covered in grass and a few small bushes. Larger plants, such as trees, rarely grow on grasslands. Grasslands are called prairies in the United States

gulf
Large area of sea that is almost enclosed by land, such as the Gulf of Mexico and Persian Gulf

hot (thermal) spring
Place where hot water, heated by volcanic activity, flows out of cracks in the ground

hurricane
Very violent storm with extremely strong winds that can cause a great deal of damage

hydroelectric power
Electricity created by machinery driven by fast-flowing water. Water forced under high pressure through dams built across rivers is often used for this purpose

iceberg
Massive piece of ice that has broken off from a glacier or ice sheet and floated out to sea

imports
Goods or services bought from another country

irrigation
Supplying water to dry areas of land, so that crops can grow there. The water is carried or pumped along pipes or ditches

island
Piece of land that has water all around it. Islands occur in oceans, seas, lakes, and rivers

lake
Large body of water surrounded by land

migrate
Move from one country or region to go and live in another. People migrate for many reasons, such as to find work or escape war

mine
Place where naturally occurring resources (such as coal, iron ore, copper, and gold) and gemstones (such as diamonds and rubies) are dug out of the ground

mineral
Natural substance found in the Earth's rocks, such as metals and precious gemstones, which are removed by mining

monsoon
Strong wind that blows across south and Southeast Asia. It changes direction as the seasons change, causing very heavy rain from May to September.

mountain
Area of land that rises up much higher than the land around it to form a peak at the top. Some mountain tops are so high that they reach the icy cold air far above Earth, and so have snow on them even in summer.

national park
Area of countryside that has been preserved in its natural state by the government of a country to protect the wildlife there and for people to enjoy.

native
Person linked to a place by birth, or whose family are from the original inhabitants of an area.

nomads
People who do not live in one fixed place. Instead they move around an area in search of food, water, and land to graze their animals on

oasis
Area of fertile land in the desert. Plants can grow easily there, unlike in the rest of the desert, because water lies on or very close to the surface

ocean
Very large sea. There are five oceans: Pacific Ocean, Atlantic Ocean, Indian Ocean, Arctic Ocean, and Southern Ocean

pampas
Name given to the vast grasslands found in part of South America

peninsula
Strip of land that is surrounded by water on three of its sides

plain
Area of flat, open land with very few trees. Plains are often covered with grass

plateau
Large area of high, flat land. Some mountains, such as Table Mountain in Cape Town, South Africa, have a plateau at the top

polar region
Area near to the North or South Pole. Polar regions are covered in a thick layer of ice for most of the year and are extremely cold

population
Total number of people living in a given area of land.

port
Town or city on the coast with a harbour, where boats and ships can load or unload goods and let passengers board or get off

province
Officially recognized area of a country or state. Provinces often have their own leaders, although they are still governed by the laws of the country they are part of

rainforest
Dense forest with very high rainfall. Most are near the Equator and are also very hot.

rapids
Part of a river that is moving at great speed, because it is flowing over very steep ground.

reservoir
Large natural or artificial lake, where water is collected and stored for people to use in homes, businesses, industry, and farming

river
Large stream of water that flows from a high place to a lower place. Rivers start as small streams high up in the mountains and flow down into the sea

safari
Journey that involves looking at wild animals in their natural surroundings. It usually refers to trips taken in Africa

savanna
Name given to open grasslands in tropical and sub-tropical countries

sea
Large body of salt water. Seas (including oceans) cover most of the Earth's surface

sea level
Average level of the surface of the world's seas and oceans. The height of land is given as how far it is above sea level. The depth of a sea or ocean is given as how far it is below sea level

shrubland
Area of land covered in lots of small trees and bushes, as well as different types of grass

species
Distinct group of animals or plants that share similar features

state
Nation or territory that is organized as a community under one government

steppe
Name given to the vast, grassy plains that stretch from Eastern Europe right across central Asia

terrain
Area of land, usually with a particular feature, such as mountains or grassy plains

territory
Area of land that belongs to a particular country or state

tornado
Spinning cloud of very strong wind. Tornadoes will destroy almost anything in their path

tribe
Group of people who share the same culture and history. It usually refers to people who live together in traditional communites, far from cities and towns

tropical
Conditions found in areas near the Equator. Tropical weather, for example, is very hot and wet

valley
Low area of land between hills or mountains

vegetation
Type of plants found in an area of land

volcano
Mountain or hill that may erupt, pouring out hot lava (molten rock) from a crater in its top

wetlands
Land with wet, spongy soil, such as a marsh or swamp. Many animals and plants specialize in living in wetlands

wildlife
Wild animals that live in an area of land

INDEX

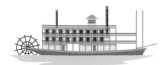

CREDITS

Dorling Kindersley would like to thank the following people for their assistance in the preparation of this book: Helen Garvey for design assistance; Emma Chafer, Jolyon Goddard, Katy Lennon, and Kathleen Teece for editorial assistance; Ann Kay for proofreading; Molly Lattin for additional illustrations

Picture Credits:
The publisher would also like to thank the following for their kind permission to reproduce their photographs:

(Key: a-above; b-below/bottom; c-centre; f-far; l-left; r-right; t-top)

10 Dorling Kindersley: Claire Cordier (br); Greg Ward / Rough Guides (cb). 11 Dorling Kindersley: Ian Cummings / Rough Guides (cr); Rowan Greenwood (tc). 12 Corbis: PCN (tc). Dorling Kindersley: Tim Draper / Rough Guides (cb); The University of Aberdeen (bl, fbl); Paul Whitfield / Rough Guides (cra). 13 Dorling Kindersley: Tim Draper / Rough Guides (c). 14 Corbis: Louie Psihoyos (cl). Dorling Kindersley: Martin Richardson / Rough Guides (tl). 16 Corbis: AS400 DB / Bettmann (db); Mauricio Ramos / Aurora Photos (da). 17 Corbis: Juan Medina / Reuters (fcr). Dorling Kindersley: Demetrio Carrasco / Rough Guides (c); Thomas Marent (tl). Dreamstime.com: Lunamarina (tc). 18 Dorling Kindersley: Greg and Yvonne Dean (tl); Tim Draper / Rough Guides (tc). 19 Alamy Images: BlueOrangeStudio (tc). Corbis: EPA / Alejandro Ernesto (cra). 20 Dorling Kindersley: Rowan Greenwood (cl). 24 Dorling Kindersley: Tim Draper / Rough Guides (cb); Thomas Marent (bl). 25 Corbis: Hagenmuller / Jean-Francois / Hemis (b). 26 Alamy Images: Maxime Dube (bc). Corbis: Philip Lee Harvey (tr). 27 Alamy Images: Florian Kopp / imageBROKER (bl). Dorling Kindersley: Cotswold Wildlife Park & Gardens, Oxfordshire, UK (fcr); Tim Draper / Rough Guides (tl); Hoa Luc (cr). 28 Corbis: Corbis / David Selman (tl); Robin Hanbury-Tenison / robertharding (tc). Dorling Kindersley: Natural History Museum, London (bc). 29 Corbis: EPA / Marius Becker (bl); Tim Tadder (tc); Tim Kiusalaas / Masterfile (cr). Fotolia: Eric Isselee (tr). Getty Images: Grant Ordelheide / Aurora Open (bc). 30 Dorling Kindersley: Tim Draper / Rough Guides (bc). 31 Alamy Images: Image Gap (bl). Corbis: Christopher Pillitz / In Pictures (cr). Dorling Kindersley: Tim Draper / Rough Guides (br). 33 Dorling Kindersley: Tim Draper / Rough Guides (cr). 36 Dorling Kindersley: Suzanne Porter / Rough Guides (b). 37 Dorling Kindersley: Rowan Greenwood (tc); Alex Robinson / Rough Guides (cr). Dreamstime.com: Roman Murushkin / Romanvm (br). 38 Dorling Kindersley: Suzanne Porter / Rough Guides (c, fbl). 39 Alamy Images: blickwinkel / Irlmeier (bc). Corbis: Kazuyoshi Nomachi (bl). Dreamstime.com: Gelia (tc). 40 Dorling Kindersley: Bolton Metro Museum (tr); Eddie Gerald / Rough Guides (db). 41 Alamy Images: Andrew McConnell / robertharding (tc). 42 Alamy Images: Images Of Africa / Gallo Images (br); Paula Smith (bc). Dorling Kindersley: Powell-Cotton Museum, Kent (cr); University of Pennsylvania Museum of Archaeology and Anthropology (tr). 43 Alamy Images:

blickwinkel (bl). Dorling Kindersley: Barnabas Kindersley (cra), Roger Dixon (ca). 44 Corbis: Per-Anders Pettersson (cl); Dr. Richard Roscoe / Visuals Unlimited (tc); Olivier Polet (br). 45 Alamy Images: Liam West (tr). Corbis: Paul Souders (bc). 47 Alamy Images: Zute Lightfoot (cra). Corbis: Foodfolio / the food passionates (bl). 48 Alamy Images: Chad Ehlers (cl); Emmanuel Lattes (crb); robertharding (bl). Dorling Kindersley: Greg Roden / Rough Guides (tr); Tim Draper / Rough Guides (db). Dreamstime.com: Bin Zhou / Dropu (br). Fotolia: Galyna Andrushko (bc). PunchStock: Digital Vision (cb). 54 Corbis: Creativ Studio Heinemann / Westend61 (br); Dave G. Houser (tc). Dreamstime.com: Klikk (cl). 55 Dorling Kindersley: Roger Norum / Rough Guides (tc); Helena Smith / Rough Guides (cr). 56 Corbis: Iain Masterton / incamerastock (cl). 58 Dorling Kindersley: Angus Osborn / Rough Guides (da). Fotolia: Zee (db). 59 Dorling Kindersley: Paris Tourist Office (c). 60 Dorling Kindersley: Herge / Les Editions Casterman (db); Greg Ward / Rough Guides (bl); Dreamstime: Travelpeter (br). 61 Alamy Images: Realimage (br). Corbis: Werner Dieterich / Westend61 (cl). 62 Alamy Images: Amt Haug / LOOK Die Bildagentur der Fotografen GmbH (bc); Hans P. Szyszka / Novarc Images (da). 63 Corbis: Jon Hicks (tl). 65 Corbis: Hugh Sitton (bc). Dreamstime.com: Netfalls (tr). 66 Corbis: Rolf Bruderer / Blend Images (br); The Gallery Collection (tl). Dorling Kindersley: James McConnachie / Rough Guides (tr); Scootopia (cl). 67 Alamy Images: amphotos (bc). Dorling Kindersley: Jon Cunningham / Rough Guides (c). 68 Dorling Kindersley: Jon Cunningham / Rough Guides (c); Helena Smith / Rough Guides (cl). 69 Dorling Kindersley: Barnabas Kindersley (cra). 70 Dorling Kindersley: Tim Draper / Rough Guides (bl, bc); Eddie Gerald / Rough Guides (tr); Michelle Grant / Rough Guides (fcrb). 71 Alamy Images: Viktor Onyshchenko (bl). 72 Dorling Kindersley: Gregory Wrona / Rough Guides (tl, tr). 75 Dorling Kindersley: Chris Christoforou / Rough Guides (tl); Michelle Grant / Rough Guides (bc). 76 Alamy Stock Photo: Douglas Lander (cb). 77 Alamy Stock Photo: Lisovskaya Natalia / The Picture Pantry (bl). Alamy Stock Photo: Iain Masterton (tl). 79 Dorling Kindersley: Roger Norum / Rough Guides (tr). 82 Corbis: Earl & Nazima Kowall (cl); George Steinmetz (tc); Jochen Schlenker / robertharding (bl). 83 Corbis: Tuul & Bruno Morandi (tr); Jose Fuste Raga (cr). Dorling Kindersley: Tim Draper / Rough Guides (br). 84 Alamy Images: Nurlan Kalchinov (cl). Corbis: Gavin Hellier / JAI (br); Jose Fuste Raga (tr). 85 Alamy Images: NASA (t). Corbis: Robert Jean / Hemis (bl). Dorling Kindersley: Blackpool Zoo, Lancashire, UK (br). 86 Dorling Kindersley: Lydia Evans / Rough Guides (tr). 90 Dorling Kindersley: University of Pennsylvania Museum of Archaeology and Anthropology (cl, cb/bull, cb/necklace, bc). 91 Alamy Images: ArkReligion.com / Art Directors & TRIP (cr); Dario Bajurin (br). 92 Alamy Images: Danita Delimont (db); George Rutter (tr); Farhad Hashimi (da). 93 Alamy Images: Ali Mujtaba (cl). Dreamstime.com: Dragoneye (tr). 94 Corbis: Philippe Lissac / Godong (cl). Dorling Kindersley: Dave Abram / Rough Guides (ca).

95 Dorling Kindersley: Archives du 7e Art / Ashutosh Gowariker Productions / Photos 12 (bl); Tim Draper / Rough Guides (tl); Gavin Thomas / Rough Guides (ca); Natural History Museum, London (fcr/amethyst). 96 Alamy Images: Thornton Cohen (fcr). Dorling Kindersley: Tim Draper / Rough Guides (tc, fcl). 97 Dorling Kindersley: Liberty's Owl, Raptor and Reptile Centre, Hampshire, UK (br). 98 Dorling Kindersley: Karen Trist / Rough Guides (c). Fotolia: Eric Isselee (bl). Getty Images: Ltd, Imagemore Co. (bc). National Geographic Creative: O. Louis Mazzatenta (tr). 99 Corbis: Peter Langer / Design Pics (tl). Dorling Kindersley: Alan Hills / The Trustees of the British Museum (tr); Brice Minnigh / Rough Guides (fcrb). 100 Corbis: KCNA / epa (bc). 101 Dorling Kindersley: Tim Draper / Rough Guides (tc, br). 102 Alamy Images: Thomas Frey / imageBROKER (br); Horizon Images / Motion (cl). Corbis: Adam / photocuisine (tl); Jeremy Woodhouse / Masterfile (tr). Dorling Kindersley: Durham University Oriental Museum (db). 103 Corbis: Stefano Politi Markovina / JAI (bl). Dreamstime.com: Craig Hanson / Rssfhs (tc). 104 Dorling Kindersley: Tim Draper / Rough Guides (ftl, fcla). 105 Dorling Kindersley: Simon Bracken / Rough Guides (tc); Museum of the Moving Image, London (br). 106 Dorling Kindersley: Sean Hunter Photography (cl). 107 Dorling Kindersley: Simon Bracken / Rough Guides (crb); Sarah Cummins / Rough Guides (cl); Suzanne Porter / Rough Guides (db); Jean-Christophe Godet / Rough Guides (bc); Tim Draper / Rough Guides (br). 111 Corbis: Laurie Chamberlain (br); Frans Lanting (tc); Pete Oxford / Minden Pictures (tr). 113 Corbis: Claire Leimbach / robertharding (cra). Dorling Kindersley: Sydney Opera House Trust / Jamie Marshall (crb). Dreamstime.com: Callan Chesser / Ewanchesser (br); Bin Zhou / Dropu (tr). 114 Corbis: Steve Christo / Steve Christo Photography (da). Dorling Kindersley: Pitt Rivers Museum, University of Oxford (tr). 115 Alamy Images: travellinglight (tl). Dorling Kindersley: Paul Whitfield / Rough Guides (ca, bl). 116 Dreamstime.com: Staphy (db). Getty Images: Frank Krahmer / Photographer's Choice RF (fbl). Science Photo Library: British Antarctic Survey (fcl). 117 Alamy Images: Classic Image (cr). NASA: U.S. Antarctic Search for Meteorites (ANSMET) (tr). 118 Dorling Kindersley: The University of Aberdeen (tl); Jerry Young (fcl). 119 Alamy: Chad Ehlers (tr). Dorling Kindersley: Roger Norum / Rough Guides (cr); Pitt Rivers Museum, University of Oxford (br).

All other images © Dorling Kindersley

For further information see: www.dkimages.com